GOD IS IN THE SMALL STUFF

for changing times

Let God Help You
Thrive in a
Difficult World

BRUCE & STAN

BARBOUR
PUBLISHING

ISBN 978-1-61626-529-8

Published by Barbour Publishing, Inc., P.O. Box 719, Uhrichsville, Ohio 44683, www.barbourbooks.com

Our mission is to publish and distribute inspirational products offering exceptional value and biblical encouragement to the masses.

Member of the
Evangelical Christian
Publishers Association

Printed in the United States of America.

Contents

Introduction 5

1. Be Joyful When Trials Come 9
2. Ask God for Wisdom 15
3. Believe and Don't Doubt 21
4. Keep Money in Perspective 27
5. Persevere under Trial 33
6. God Won't Tempt You 39
7. God Never Changes 45
8. Don't Get Angry in a Hurry 51
9. Do What God Says 57
10. Hold Your Tongue 63
11. Take Care of the Orphans and Widows 69
12. Don't Show Favoritism 75
13. Love Your Neighbor 81
14. Keep All of God's Commands 87
15. Mercy Triumphs over Judgment 93
16. Faith without Action Is Dead 99
17. Belief in God Is Not Enough 105
18. Your Faith Is Not Alone 111
19. The Burden of Teaching 117
20. Small Things Make a Big Difference 123

21. The Power of the Tongue 129
22. Are You Praising or Cursing? 135
23. The Humility of Wisdom 141
24. The Problem with Earthly Wisdom 147
25. The Benefits of Heavenly Wisdom 153
26. The Reason You Don't Have 159
27. Don't Be God's Enemy 165
28. Humble Yourself 171
29. Submit to God and Resist the Devil 177
30. Come Near to God 183
31. A Time for Mourning 189
32. Who Are You to Judge? 195
33. Nobody Knows What Tomorrow Will Bring 201
34. Doing God's Will 207
35. The Perverted Power of Wealth 213
36. Be Patient until the Lord Comes 219
37. Stop Your Grumbling 225
38. The Rewards of Perseverance 231
39. Let Your Word Be Your Bond 237
40. Pray for Healing 241
41. How to Pray with Power 247
42. Bring Back a Wandering Soul 253
    Notes/About Bruce and Stan 256

Introduction

There was a time when tough things came and went. Wars? Recessions? Natural disasters? Most people can remember when such difficulties had a beginning *and* an end. The problems would start, there would be a period of struggle, then recovery would follow—giving people a chance to catch their collective breath.

That doesn't seem to be the case anymore. Something has happened, a shift that makes our world very different from former times. In a word, the times we live in are *changing*—and it doesn't seem that things are going to go back to the safe, secure, and predictable way we used to know. Wars, economic difficulties, political unrest, and natural disasters—which used to occur in cycles—now show signs of being chronic. In other words, it seems as though they are here to stay.

So what do you do in the face of unending pressures that create tension now and uncertainty in the future, making your life that much more stressful? In our view, there is only one thing to do: turn to the one true God—who is the same yesterday, today, and tomorrow—and to God's eternal Word, the Bible.

That's why we wrote this book (and we hope it's why you picked it up). Like you, we've been feeling the pressure of these changing times. And because we know from experience and from the Bible that God is very much involved in our lives and our world, we firmly believe that God is someone we all can count on in these chronically challenging days—no matter how big or small our problems may be. Or, to frame it in the title of this book, "*God is in the small stuff for changing times.*"

We've written a number of God Is in the Small Stuff books, and many people around the world have told us how much they appreciate the underlying message of each one: *stop worrying and invite God into the details of your life.* The theme of this book is the same but with a twist. This time we decided to take you straight to the Bible—specifically to the New Testament letter of James—to share some remarkable truths we have learned about the way God reassures, encourages, and teaches people who are going through stress-filled changing times.

You see, people in the first century (when James wrote his letter) were very much like us. Okay, so they weren't *exactly* like us, since most of them were Jewish Christians, but their experiences and life circumstances were very similar to ours. They were going through a variety of trials—economic difficulties, a worldwide famine, oppression from powerful people, and a general feeling that God wasn't paying attention to them. Knowing their situation, James filled his letter with practical advice that means as much to us today as it did to those believers two millennia ago:

- Appreciate your trials when they come.

- Ask for wisdom when faced with tough decisions.

- Help others when you are tempted to ignore them.

- Remain civil and loving in a culture that is becoming more combative.

- Trust God for all things.

- Remain faithful to God no matter what.

- Learn how to pray with power.

As you read through the letter James wrote and the 42 chapters in this book, our hope and prayer is that you will invite God into the details of your life, the big and small, the bad and good. In these changing times, none of us can do it alone. We need one another, and we need the Lord, "the Father of the heavenly lights, who does not change like shifting shadows" (James 1:17).

Bruce & Stan

Consider it pure joy, my brothers and sisters,
whenever you face trials of many kinds,
because you know that the testing of your faith
produces perseverance.

JAMES 1:2–3

ONE

Be Joyful
When Trials Come

Everybody loves a good comeback story. It's what Hollywood thrives on. Give a film director a great tale of someone who fell to the lowest of lows only to claw his or her way back to the highest heights, and you may just have a blockbuster on your hands. We love hearing about the slum dog who becomes a millionaire. We pull for the disgraced athlete who becomes a champion. We are brought to tears by the perseverance of the child who battles back from cancer.

Even though these rags-to-riches stories are truly inspirational, the reality is that most of us will never experience such extreme ups and downs. Most of us live lives that are not filled with extraordinary events. Instead, our lives consist of ordinary ebbs and flows interspersed with wonderful experiences as well as "trials of many kinds" that are part of the normal course of life.

That's right. It's *normal* to face trials in your life, just as it's normal to experience blessings. The big difference, of course, is that with blessings, it's easy to be happy and grateful and full of joy. With trials, not so much. In fact, your first impulse in the face of difficulty, uncertainty, and disruption—in short, *trials*—may be the exact opposite of joy. Rather than welcoming a particular challenge in your life, you probably have a tendency to be frustrated, resentful, confused, or even angry. We all do! But those aren't the emotional responses God wants us to have. If we truly believe that God uses everything in our lives—the trials, as well as the blessings—for our benefit, then we need to take a different approach.

Simply put, we need to see our trials and troubles as the means to an end, with the end being a stronger and more productive faith. You've no doubt heard the expression "No pain, no gain." That pretty much sums up what James is talking about here. Without the trials that inevitably come into our lives, usually when we least expect them, we have a tendency to become satisfied and self-sufficient. When times are going well, it's easy to reduce our dependency on God. But when trials come, it's amazing how close we get to God. We pray more, read the Bible more, even go to church more. We get to where God wants us. That's why sometimes God is the one who makes life difficult for us. He wants our attention, and He loves us too much to let us stay where we are.

> *My child, don't reject the Lord's discipline,*
> *and don't be upset when he corrects you.*
> *For the Lord corrects those he loves, just as a*
> *father corrects a child in whom he delights.*
>
> PROVERBS 3:11–12 NLT

It's not easy to feel joyful when you're going through a trial or a time of testing. That's why James instructs us to "consider it pure joy" when we face trials. When we feel like responding in a different way, we need to consider the outcome or end result that comes from going through a trial. James says it plainly: the test will produce perseverance. And it isn't just any perseverance; it's a perseverance tied to faith. When the circumstances around you are changing, especially in these days of shifts and uncertainties, the first thing that should come to mind is the steadfastness of your faith in God.

Whenever waves of doubt and concern threaten to overcome you in times of trouble, remember that God is your solid Rock, who promises to see you through, no matter how difficult your trial, test, or temptation.

> *No test or temptation that comes your way is beyond the course of what others have had to face. All you need to remember is that God will never let you down; he'll never let you be pushed past your limit; he'll always be there to help you come through it.*
>
> 1 CORINTHIANS 10:13 MSG

- Resist the temptation to choose the easy path in life.

- It's easier to be happy with blessings than with trials, but trials are more likely to lead to joy.

- If you choose to reject God's discipline now, you may not have a choice later.

- Never forget that God disciplines those He loves, and it's always for your own good.

- Perseverance is impossible without faith, and faith is impossible without God.

If any of you lacks wisdom, you should ask God,
who gives generously to all without finding fault,
and it will be given to you.

JAMES 1:5

TWO

ASK GOD FOR WISDOM

One definition of *insanity* is to repeat what you have done in the past expecting different results. But if ever there was a time when we needed different results, it is now.

The tumultuous changes of the recent past have altered everything that we could count on for stability in our lives. Nothing is as it was before. You can't manage your finances with any realistic expectation of a return on your investment or even a return *of* your investment. There is no guarantee that you can keep your job or that getting further education will help you get a job. The long-standing American dream of homeowner status is a nightmare for many people, all of whom would gladly walk away from their residential albatross, if only they could. Even the certainty of Social Security at retirement is becoming increasingly illusory with the designated "retirement age" continually increasing and the government spending money faster than it can be printed. The tried-and-true principal that most problems can be solved with hard work no longer applies when there is no work to be had.

There is no shortage of advice to help us adapt to these changing times. But advice is nothing more than an opinion stated with conviction. We're swirling in a sea of opinions, information, recommendations, and cautions. What we really need is wisdom to choose our next steps.

Wisdom picks up where mere information leaves off. Wisdom is the ability to discern the best course of action based on the information available. Of course, trusting our own wisdom—or the wisdom of the so-called experts—may not be the best option. After all, it was our own wisdom and the experts who got us into our current mess. It is time to go to the ultimate source of wisdom—God Himself.

Let's face it. God's wisdom transcends any of the psychobabble or talk-show hype that is propounded by the media or well-intentioned family and friends:

*"My thoughts are nothing like your thoughts," says
the Lord. "And my ways are far beyond anything
you could imagine. For just as the heavens are higher
than the earth, so my ways are higher than your
ways and my thoughts higher than your thoughts."*

ISAIAH 55:8–9 NLT

It shouldn't surprise us that God-wisdom is better
credentialed than anything from another source. After all,
God has the advantage of being all knowing, and His résumé
lists His accomplishment of creating the entire universe. But
perhaps best of all, God knows you on a deeply personal and
intimate basis:

*"Your heavenly Father already knows all your
needs."*

MATTHEW 6:32 NLT

Is God hiding His wisdom from you or making it difficult to ascertain? Absolutely not! In fact, He is eager to reveal
it to you. All you need to do is ask Him for it. He will share it
with you, and He will give it to you in generous portions.

Individually and as a society we've tried to make life work according to our own rules. We fooled ourselves for a long time, but now much of life has come crashing in on us like a house of cards. Nothing seems to work anymore. Everything seems broken with no hope of repair.

It is time for us to live life with a new approach and a different understanding. God's wisdom needs to be applied to our current circumstances. He's ready to reveal that wisdom to you. Ask Him for it.

- *Human wisdom* is an oxymoron. If you don't think so, you don't get out much.

- God's ways are wiser than man's ways.

- You don't have to follow God's advice, but if you turn a deaf ear to Him, you'll have to suffer the consequences.

- God wants to share His wisdom with you freely and generously. You can't beat that quality or that price.

- You've tried life your way; now try life God's way.

*But when you ask, you must believe and not doubt,
because the one who doubts is like a wave of the sea,
blown and tossed by the wind.*

JAMES 1:6

THREE

BELIEVE AND DON'T DOUBT

Nowadays people are asking God for a lot of stuff, both big and small. In these changing times when everything seems to be shifting—the economy, technology, the climate, relationships, politics, values, and the culture in general—it's only natural that people are asking God for help.

Makes sense, doesn't it? When things around you are shifting and shaky, you need stability. That's God, the Rock (see Psalm 71:3). When the world seems to be changing, you need God more than ever, because He is the one who does not change (see James 1:17). When the bottom is falling out of your finances, who better to help you than Jehovah Jireh, the great provider (see Genesis 22:14)? But what if you've been crying out to God, calling on His name, praying and pleading, and all you can hear is the echo of your own voice? Is there something wrong with the way you're asking God? Or is it that He just doesn't want to answer?

These are great questions to be asking in changing times, and fortunately James gives some wise advice that will help you arrive at some answers. Specifically, he gives us two conditions essential for getting results. (Spoiler alert: what we're about to share with you has nothing to do with getting God to do anything you want. God isn't a vending machine.)

The first condition for asking is *belief*, not belief in God—that's a given—but belief that God is able and willing to take care of you in every detail. This is what Jesus meant when He said:

> *"If that is how God clothes the grass of the field,*
> *which is here today and tomorrow is thrown into the*
> *fire, will he not much more clothe you—you of little*
> *faith? So do not worry, saying, 'What shall we eat?'*
> *or 'What shall we drink?' or 'What shall we wear?'*
> *For the pagans run after all these things, and your*
> *heavenly Father knows that you need them."*
>
> MATTHEW 6:30–32

The second condition for asking God is *confidence.* When you ask, are you confident in God's ability to give you those things He has promised, or do you doubt His love and goodness and care for you? Are you going through a tough situation in these changing times, but you're afraid to ask God for specific help because you doubt His ability to provide? A person who doubts is like "a wave of the sea, blown and tossed by the wind." When you doubt, you stop trusting God and start worrying about the results. Then you feel guilty, so you trust again, but then you go right back to worrying. It's a difficult and frustrating place to be because you're never at peace. You're being buffeted back and forth because you're double-minded, unstable, and unsettled.

How do you get out of this vicious cycle? How about asking God, before you ask for anything else, to strengthen your faith? Jesus once told a father whose child was very sick, "All things are possible for one who believes" (Mark 9:23 ESV). The father immediately cried out, "I believe; help my unbelief!" (Mark 9:24 ESV). That's what you need to do the moment you are tempted to doubt and worry. Ask God to help your unbelief. Then, as God strengthens your belief in His ability to provide, trust Him for the results. It's okay to pray specifically for what you need, but keep your eyes off the results and keep them on the Lord. Pray with open hands, trusting that God will give you what is best for you, whether that's what you asked for or not.

When you pray and ask God for something, pray like Jesus did, who simply said, "Not my will, but yours be done" (Luke 22:42). No matter what your circumstances, no matter what is going on around you, when you ask with confidence because you are focusing on God's ability rather than the results you want, God will give you what you truly need.

. . .For Changing Times

- Ask God for anything, but be aware of how you are asking. It makes a big difference in the outcome.

- The distance between confidence in God and worrying about the results is very short.

- God doesn't hesitate to give to us, but sometimes we hesitate to ask.

- If you lack confidence in God's ability to give you those things He has promised, you may be doubting God's goodness.

- The moment you are tempted to doubt and worry, ask God to strengthen your faith.

Believers in humble circumstances ought to take pride in their high position. But the rich should take pride in their humiliation—since they will pass away like a wild flower.

JAMES 1:9–10

FOUR

KEEP MONEY IN PERSPECTIVE

The Bible doesn't say anything bad about money. But it does teach that we need to watch our attitudes about it. Money is like a gun in that it can be used for the beneficial purposes of security and provision, but it can be misused for purposes of evil and destruction.

Many of us are misguided in our perspective about money. We often mistakenly think that whatever we have belongs to us, we got it by our own effort, and there is a direct correlation between how much we have and how much God loves us. But these perspectives are contrary to the biblical teachings that

- whatever we have belongs to God,

- all good things in our life come from God, and

- God's love for us is unconditional.

An incorrect perspective about money will likely give us the wrong impression about ourselves and about God's love toward us. For example, suppose you believed that your bank account balance was an accurate indicator of the amount of God's love for you. If your balance was in the negative numbers and your checks were bouncing, then you would incorrectly surmise that God had no love for you and that your economic suffering was evidence of His disdain for you. Conversely, if your account was flush and your balance had more digits than your Quicken program could accommodate, you'd erroneously believe that you actually deserved all that you acquired because God loved you more than the far less fortunate people whose misery must be attributable to their own fault.

God doesn't want money—the abundance or the lack of it—to confuse you about His love for you. If there is a danger of that happening, then God might use a change in your financial circumstances to steer your thinking back into alignment with His principles.

The recent economic implosion has caused many people to realize that they cannot take pride in their self-reliance. They might have been tempted to do so when they were sitting on a fat 401(k) plan and their home equity was multiplying exponentially. But changing times often result in a glaring glimpse of the obvious when the 401(k) plan is flat and the house is in foreclosure. All of a sudden we realize the truth: we have no ultimate control of our own financial security. Our only certainty is God's love for us and His promise to take care of our needs. He wants us to live with a humble appreciation that material possessions are transitory and that our trust should be placed in Him.

> *"So don't worry about these things, saying, 'What will we eat? What will we drink? What will we wear?' These things dominate the thoughts of unbelievers, but your heavenly Father already knows all your needs. Seek the Kingdom of God above all else, and live righteously, and he will give you everything you need."*
>
> MATTHEW 6:31–33 NLT

Conversely, whether we were in tough financial times before the economic debacle or are experiencing difficulties now because of it, God wants to raise our spiritual vision above our monetary doldrums. Your value to God is not determined by your credit rating. He loved you so much that He sent His Son to earth to pay the penalty for your sin. God desires to spend all of eternity with you. You are special to Him. He loves you for who you are, not what you own.

Don't let money obscure your view of God. When you have the correct perspective about God and His love and provision for you, only then will you be able to have the correct perspective about money.

. . .For Changing Times

- In heaven nobody will be carrying a wallet.

- Don't think you are special just because you're rich. God certainly doesn't.

- Don't think you are worthless just because you're penniless. God certainly doesn't.

- A change in your economic circumstances might be God's opportunity to change your perspective about money.

- The Bible says that God gives and God takes away. It is referring to money, not God's love.

*Blessed is the one who perseveres under trial because,
having stood the test, that person will receive the crown
of life that the Lord has promised to those who love him.*

JAMES 1:12

FIVE

PERSEVERE UNDER TRIAL

One of the most famous speeches ever given was all about perseverance under trial. World War II was raging in Europe, and Great Britain had just endured the Blitz—eight months of merciless pounding by German bombers. On October 29, 1941, British prime minister Winston Churchill visited Harrow School to speak to the students and gave a speech that would become one of the most quoted ever, mainly because it contained these inspiring words: "Never give in. Never give in. Never, never, never, never—in nothing, great or small, large or petty—never give in, except to convictions of honor and good sense. Never yield to force. Never yield to the apparently overwhelming might of the enemy."

We love those words because they get to the heart of what perseverance is all about: staying the course, standing firm, enduring. Perseverance isn't needed when things are going well, but it's absolutely necessary when you are going through trials.

Trials and tests were part of the first-century-church, just as they are in the twenty-first century. James was writing to people who were being persecuted for their faith. Many were experiencing financial hardships, and others were facing health challenges. As we go through our own challenging times, we need to remember that none of this is new. Difficult circumstances that produce hardships and suffering are part of this life on earth. Consequently, our attitude needs to be one of perseverance, not avoidance.

God never promises to keep you from those trials that test your resolve and sometimes even your faith. What He does promise is to get you through them. No matter what you're going through, God will be faithful in two specific ways. First, He will never allow you to have a burden greater than you can bear. Second, He will "provide a way out so that you can endure it" (1 Corinthians 10:13). In other words, God will help you persevere. You don't have to go through your financial difficulties, your health challenges, or your suffering alone. God will give you the courage you need to stand firm in the midst of your trials. But that's not all you can count on. Did you know there's a benefits package waiting for those who persevere? Right here in the book of James we are told what to expect.

First, the one who perseveres will be blessed, not necessarily in a physical or financial way (although that sometimes happens), but spiritually. And those spiritual blessings aren't just for this life, but for the life to come as well. That's the second benefit to those who endure and remain faithful to God when things get tough. They will receive "the crown of life." In the Greco-Roman world, a laurel wreath worn on the head was given to the victors in athletic contests. In the same sense, a crown will be given to those who suffer in this life, only the crown James is talking about is like the one Jesus promised to His followers who suffer (see Revelation 2:10).

In today's culture, athletes who win gold medals and most valuable player awards usually parlay their success into financial gain. That's not what James has in mind. This is not a what's-in-it-for-me kind of deal. This is about contemplating heavenly rewards as an encouragement for our perseverance and faithfulness. When faced with trials, temptation, and suffering in these changing times, maintaining your spiritual integrity is vital. Stay true to what you believe. Don't use your setbacks as an excuse to turn your back on God as many do. Keep your eye on the prize and "never, never, never, never—in nothing, great or small, large or petty—never give in."

. . .For Changing Times

- Perseverance isn't easy. You need God's help.

- Although God doesn't promise to keep you from experiencing trials, He does promise to get you through them—if you ask for His help.

- There has never been a time in history when Christians did not have to persevere.

- The only people who go through trials alone are those who make a deliberate choice to exclude God from their lives.

- One of the greatest benefits of the Christian life is that those who persevere through trials and difficulties will be blessed.

When tempted, no one should say, "God is tempting me."
For God cannot be tempted by evil, nor does he tempt anyone.

JAMES 1:13

SIX

GOD WON'T TEMPT YOU

No one is good at everything, but almost everyone is good at passing the blame. It started when we were young and the offenses were trivial. When interrogated by a parent about the broken lamp, we were quick to divert the blame to a sibling, a friend, or a pet. It didn't make any difference if we were a friendless only child whose pet was a goldfish. We didn't want to admit it was our own fault, so we declared that someone else was guilty.

As we grew older and our transgressions became more serious, we frequently couldn't deny wrongdoing with any sense of credibility. But that didn't mean we were any less devious. While we couldn't shift the blame for the commission of the offense, we would try to plead that we were the unwitting dupes of a more sinister mastermind: an older friend talked us into tying firecrackers to the dog's tail; a savvy older sibling told us how to sneak out of the house at night.

Decades have passed, and most of us are no longer under the parental authority that once held us accountable. But in the introspective moments of our lives, when we are trying to justify our serious transgressions to ourselves (or to a spouse or other family member), we still try to shift the responsibility. No longer is a sibling, friend, or goldfish the object of our finger-pointing. Now we have elevated the target of fault-transference to God Himself. After all, we know that there is little risk that He'll show up to defend Himself or demand that we accept full responsibility for our own screw-ups. So, while breathing a sigh of relief, as if we had been resolved of all culpability, we simply say, "Well, I did it, but it was God who tempted me in the first place."

But God has nothing to do with temptation. Ever. He is holy and sinless. It would be contrary to and prohibited by His nature to sin, so He is not affected by any temptation Himself. Nor was His Son, Jesus, the all-God, all-man incarnation of God. The Bible tells the story of Satan attempting to ensnare Jesus into sin with a series of appealing temptations. It was to no avail. God cannot sin, and He is not tempted by it.

But God's aversion to sin is not limited to His own resistance to it. His nature is so holy that He cannot and will not have any role in prompting us to sin. He is eager to forgive our sins, but He is not in the business of trying to entrap us in sin so that we are forced to ask for His forgiveness.

It we want a fall guy for the blame associated with our transgressions, it would be more accurate to blame Satan. He wants us to sin, and he will devise circumstances to facilitate it. Unlike God, Satan is not all knowing, so he doesn't have a supernatural power to know in advance what temptations we are most vulnerable to. But Satan is a great historian, and he knows what temptations have ensnared us in the past. So, based on our past performance, he is likely to repeat whatever scenario has the greatest probability of "success" from his standpoint (which is "failure" from our standpoint).

But it would be naive to blame everything on Satan. The best he can do is put the bread crumbs on the trail that leads down the pathway to sin. It is our own self-desire that causes us to cram those bread crumbs into our mouth as we barrel down the path—all the way knowing where the path leads.

We shouldn't blame God for temptation in our lives. He has nothing to do with it. It is more likely that we have put ourselves in a place of temptation, and by blaming God we're ignoring the fact that it is our decision to stay there or move out.

. . .FOR CHANGING TIMES

- The best time to think about God is *before* you cave into temptation, rather than *after* you have blown it.

- God is willing to forgive your sin if you acknowledge that it is your fault, not His. But the forgiveness of your sin doesn't mean you'll be relieved of all consequences.

- God will never tempt you to sin, but Satan is an expert at it.

- Satan gets blamed for a lot of things that he had nothing to do with.

- God may allow tough times in our lives, but we are the ones who determine if the circumstances will be manipulated into a temptation for us to sin.

Every good and perfect gift is from above,
coming down from the Father of the heavenly lights,
who does not change like shifting shadows.

JAMES 1:17

SEVEN

GOD NEVER CHANGES

If there's one thing we need in these changing times, it's the assurance that we can count on something that doesn't change. It used to be that you could count on a lot of things that didn't change. People would work in careers for the same employer for 25 or 30 years, get a pension and a gold watch, and comfortably retire. Couples would get married and stay that way for 40 or 50 years. People would go to one church for decades and have the same pastor for years.

That kind of constancy and predictability is from a bygone era. Today we change jobs and even careers multiple times, often out of necessity. Couples have different attitudes toward marriage, evidenced by growing numbers of people who choose to remain unmarried, even if they are living with another person. The faithful are leaving church in greater numbers than ever. And we haven't even mentioned the changes going on in politics, the climate, and technology.

Some change is good. Change that leads to correction or progress is necessary for growth. But when everything in your world is changing, you need an anchor to hold you steady in the middle of the storm. You need something or someone you can count on to be the same yesterday, today, and tomorrow.

There's only one "someone" you can count on to be unchanging, and that's God. In fact, immutability (the property of not changing) is one of God's characteristics (along with love, holiness, justice, and omnipotence, just to name a few). James recognized this quality in God. Even more, he experienced it firsthand as the half brother of Jesus. He saw with his own eyes how Jesus acted day after day, subject to the same interruptions and temptations that we all face, but without sin and without changing.

James makes it clear, using beautifully poetic language, that God is "the Father of the heavenly lights, who does not change like shifting shadows." God is light, and in Him there is no darkness or change. By contrast, shadows live in the dark and are always changing. Where would you rather live—in the light or in darkness? In these times of shifting shadows, we need to choose to live in the light, with God as our heavenly guide.

And God isn't just the light. He is the Father of the heavenly lights—the sun, the moon, and the stars. The connection to immutability is vivid. Unlike man-made lights that break or eventually lose their power, these heavenly lights are the same day after day, year after year, millennia after millennia. "The sun'll come out tomorrow," goes the song. The moon will be in its place, and the stars are the same today as they were 3,000 years go when King David walked out on his balcony at night and gazed up at the starry sky, prompting him to write:

> *The heavens declare the glory of God; the skies*
> *proclaim the work of his hands.*
>
> PSALM 19:1

God is above the heavens. He is the creator of the universe and everything in it. He is vaster than we can imagine, yet He is so close to you that He knows everything about you, down to the number of hairs on your head. God knows what you are going through and promises to be with you in your deepest valley, as well as on your highest mountaintop.

That the Father of heavenly lights cares about you may be difficult to understand. Even David was perplexed that someone so vast would think about us:

> *When I look at the night sky and see the work of your*
> *fingers—the moon and the stars you set in place—*
> *what are mere mortals that you should think about*
> *them, human beings that you should care for them?*
>
> PSALM 8:3–4 NLT

It's hard to understand but easy to accept. The unchanging God wants to be your rock and your salvation during these changing times.

. . .For Changing Times

- In an era of change, we need some things we can count on.

- Even more, we need someone we can count on.

- Every so often we need to think about the immensity of God.

- Thinking about God's immensity keeps our humanity in perspective.

- God's predictability provides comfort for our souls and an anchor for our storms.

My dear brothers and sisters, take note of this: Everyone should be quick to listen, slow to speak and slow to become angry.

JAMES 1:19

EIGHT

Don't Get Angry in a Hurry

It has been said that God gave us two ears and only one mouth because He wants us to listen twice as much as we talk. The notion of two mouths would destroy the symmetry of facial design and construction, so it is doubtful that God ever seriously considered it. But the ratio of speaking half as much as listening does have a biblical basis.

James had several issues that would set him off on a rant. One of his hot buttons was the immorality caused by our uncontrolled and unguarded verbal comments. His code term for this problem was *the tongue*. He was following the custom used throughout the Bible in which the tongue is associated with the content of our speech:

I said to myself, "I will watch what I do and not
sin in what I say. I will hold my tongue when the
ungodly are around me."

PSALM 39:1 NLT

While James doesn't give us a 2:1 ratio of listening to speaking, he does indicate that a priority should be given to listening. He says that we should listen *first* and speak *second*. We should have a preference for listening. We should listen a lot and listen well. In fact, he wants us to be *quick* to listen. We should be prompt about it. Listening should be our utmost concern.

But James doesn't want us to rush the listening in order to get to our turn at talking. Yes, responding can occur after we have listened first and well. But even after we have listened fully, we might need to delay our response. James wants us to be *slow* to speak.

James wasn't a stickler about all of this merely for the sake of conversational etiquette. His cautions about listening and speaking are all given in the context of preserving personal relationships that could otherwise be jeopardized by unbridled comments uttered in anger. His principles apply whether the conversations are between spouses or parents and children in the home, or between others in the workplace, in the neighborhood, or at church. James intends to give us practical advice for ensuring that our conversation is consistent with Christ's command to love our neighbors as we love ourselves (see Mark 12:31).

The deliberate restraint of listening before responding is particularly relevant to us during times of turmoil. When times are tough or uncertain or stressful, we are on edge. When the world is changing around us and we are operating without a sense of security, fear takes over. We become short tempered, and our natural tendency is to lash out rather than take the approach that James suggests.

Think of the proverbial man who comes home from work and kicks his dog. He is not angry at the dog. He is angry and frustrated by his circumstances at work. The dog is merely an unwitting target. And so it will be with anyone who crosses our path during troubling times in our lives. And who is most likely to cross your path? A spouse, a child, a friend, a neighbor, or a coworker. You won't be mad at the person, but he or she will be an easy target for your anger. This is precisely why James couples the precaution to be "slow to become angry" with his directive to be "slow to speak." We need to restrain our speaking in order to give our anger a longer fuse.

Being quick to listen and slow to speak is a principle that will serve us well at any time. But these are particularly wise words to guide our conversations when we are under the stress of changing times that put a strain on our attitude and affect our relationships.

- A word withheld is better than a word uttered in anger.

- Don't merely hear someone. Listen to what he or she is saying.

- It is difficult to yell at someone if you keep your mouth closed.

- If someone is angry with you, let him or her speak first. When the person is finished, say, "Please tell me more." This will give you time to cool down, and it will confuse the other person.

- The purpose of listening is to gain an understanding of the other person's perspective. Be more concerned with relating to his or her perspective than trying to defend yourself.

Do not merely listen to the word, and so deceive yourselves. Do what it says.

JAMES 1:22

NINE

Do What God Says

Wouldn't you just love to know God's will for your life? We're not talking about the big-picture will of God, which is for everyone to have a relationship with Him (see 2 Peter 3:9). This is about the detailed parts of your life: what you should do in this or that situation, the kind of career you should pursue, how to deal with the financial stress you are under, what to do when someone you love gets really sick—stuff like that. Wouldn't you like to know what God wants you to do in those kinds of situations?

We all would, and we all can! We can know God's will for our lives every day by doing something every day, something that is so simple, yet so profound and so surefire, that it comes with a guarantee. Here it is: *you can know God's will by reading God's Word and doing what it says.*

Of course, that's easier said than done, which is why so many people run around worried and wondering if they are in God's will. They may *hear* or *read* God's Word, but they don't *do* what it says. Big mistake! Not just because they miss out on knowing God's will, but because they also miss out on God's blessing.

James gets right to the point when he says, "If you listen to the Word but don't do what it says, you are lying to yourself" (authors' paraphrase). You are like a person who looks in a mirror, sees a familiar face, then walks away and forgets what he or she looks like. That seems like an impossibility, which is exactly the point. To forget what you look like, you'd have to be self-deluded. You'd just be fooling yourself.

Likewise, when you read the Bible—which is full of thousands of guidelines and commands meant to show you how to live a flourishing life that pleases God—and then fail to do what it says, you are just fooling yourself. Worse, you are living outside of God's will. That's because God's will is pretty much contained in God's Word. No hocus-pocus, no wondering and worrying. If you want to know God's will, know God's Word and do what it says.

Now, at this point, you may be wondering about the small

stuff in your life you need help with. The Bible doesn't cover everything you need to know, does it? Well, yes, it does cover everything, if by *everything* you mean everything that's important. The apostle Paul lays out the ways God's Word does this:

> *All Scripture is God-breathed and is useful for*
> *teaching, rebuking, correcting and training in*
> *righteousness, so that the servant of God may be*
> *thoroughly equipped for every good work.*
> 2 TIMOTHY 3:16–17

When you take those two verses phrase by phrase, you can see the detailed way in which God helps you make good decisions while helping you sort out the bad ones. On top of that, you can trust the Bible to deliver trustworthy advice and counsel. Here's why.

First of all, the Bible isn't just another self-help book. It's written by men who were directly inspired by God in every detail. You can trust the Bible because God is completely responsible for its content. Second, the Bible will teach you, help you stay out of trouble, and correct you when you stray from God's will. Finally, the Bible sets your spiritual agenda. When you read it faithfully and do what it says, you will be a competent Christian, prepared and qualified to do "every good work" God wants you to do. Even more, when you live in God's will by doing what He asks you to do, you will be blessed in what you do. That's the guarantee.

Oh, it may not be in ways you think are appropriate (usually material blessings come to mind first, something God considers but doesn't always deliver), but God's blessings will always be in ways He knows are best for you, especially in these changing times.

- Everyone wants to know God's will, but not everyone wants to do it.

- Knowing that God's Word contains God's will should motivate us to read and study the Bible diligently. So why don't we?

- Don't fool yourself into thinking you are pleasing God without doing what His Word tells you to do.

- God's Word isn't just good; it's good for you.

- The Bible may not be a self-help book, but you will definitely help yourself when you read it and do what it says.

Those who consider themselves religious and yet do not keep a tight rein on their tongues deceive themselves, and their religion is worthless.

JAMES 1:26

TEN

HOLD YOUR TONGUE

We often rely on indicators when it is difficult to get an accurate reading of a certain condition that is not readily apparent. For example, we look at a gas gauge to determine the amount of fuel in our vehicle's tank. Even though we can sense the outside temperature and know whether it is generally hot or cold, we look at a thermometer to get a precise measurement in Fahrenheit degrees. And we get a blood test to discover our cholesterol numbers.

It is unfortunate that there is no gauge to determine the sincerity of our faith. Oh, wait a minute. James says that there is such an indicator—our tongue. He says that the authenticity of our faith in God is revealed by our ability to constrain our speech when we would otherwise be tempted to issue a verbal blast at someone. More precisely, James says that our religious hypocrisy is exposed when we don't control our speech.

Notice the descriptive language James uses:

Those who consider themselves religious and yet do not keep a tight rein on their tongues deceive themselves, and their religion is worthless.

JAMES 1:26

James is saying that the tongue is like a wild stallion that can be controlled only by a bit and reins. If we do not hold a tight rein on our tongues, they will run wild and may cause damage. For the protection of others and ourselves, we need to keep our tongues controlled.

Don't miss the fact that James is talking about people who already consider themselves to be religious. But to James's way of thinking, they are frauds. They might be using their tongues at times to say all of the proper and acceptable religious verbiage. They might be quick to quote Bible verses. They sprinkle their conversations with "God bless you" and "I'll pray for you." Their prayers might be so eloquent that you think you're listening to a Shakespearean soliloquy. But this is just their phony side.

In reality, these people don't have a sincere faith. When they aren't in "religious" mode, they are the people who are spreading gossip and telling lies. They are eager to spread rumors and enjoy the controversy that their comments cause. James says the faith of such people is worthless from God's perspective. They are hypocrites to such a degree that they don't even realize that their "faith" is phony. But it is. Their whole religious life is a sham, and there is no heaven in their future, even though they talk about the mansion that's waiting for them there.

Notice that James does not say that they are disqualified from God's salvation because of their unbridled tongue. Nor have they lost their salvation because of their lying and rumors. His point is that their continued refusal to try to "keep a tight rein on their tongues" is proof that they never had a truly sincere faith and commitment to God in the first place.

This is an indicator that you can use in your own life to take a gut check on the sincerity of your personal faith in God. If you are going through uncertain and changing times, take this opportunity to check the indicator, the reading of which might be below normal since we often lose the ability to maintain the "religious" disguise when times get tough. You don't need to achieve perfection in controlling your tongue. But you'll want to determine if you are making an effort to hold tight on the reins.

- A religious disguise might fool others, but it won't fool God. Be careful that you aren't fooling yourself.

- The damage that can be caused by your tongue will be greatly disproportionate to its size. A few small words can do great damage.

- Don't evaluate the sincerity of your faith by the religious things you say. Evaluate the authenticity of your faith by the things you say that are not Christlike.

- You need to guard your tongue the most when times are tough.

- What is in your heart is often revealed by what comes out of your mouth.

Religion that is pure and undefiled before God, the Father, is this: to visit orphans and widows in their affliction, and to keep oneself unstained from the world.

JAMES 1:27 ESV

ELEVEN

TAKE CARE OF THE
ORPHANS AND WIDOWS

If there's one constant in these changing times, it's this: the poor, the disadvantaged, the marginalized, and the oppressed are everywhere. In past recessions and even during the Great Depression in the 1930s, the poor were very visible in unemployment and soup lines. But, in the past, many of the poor had the opportunity to improve themselves once the dark financial clouds had given way to economic sunshine.

These days the clouds appear more menacing and more global than ever before, and the prospect for clearing seems to be dimmer. For many, the economic storm may never pass, especially if they live in a third-world country.

That's the other thing that's different about these changing times. Because of the vast and sophisticated communication systems in place, the global poor and oppressed are as close to us as our computers and smartphones. In past generations, people were aware of the poor in their cities. They generally knew where the poor lived and did their best to avoid those neighborhoods. But poor people in other countries were so remote that the privileged never gave them a second thought, unless it was to pray for them in a generalized manner, something like, "Lord, we pray for all the starving people in China." Nobody knew for sure if there were starving people in China, but with such a big and mysterious country, it had to be true!

We don't have the excuse of ignorance any longer. We see the suffering of refugees in Africa, of wounded and displaced earthquake victims in Haiti, of oppressed citizens in North Korea. More immediately, we are aware of the poor in our own communities because churches and parachurch organizations like the Salvation Army tell us exactly what is going on, and it isn't good.

If you've struggled financially in these changing times, you know the feeling and the stigma of living on the edge. On the other hand, if God has blessed you with steady employment and a roof over your head, you have the opportunity to help the disadvantaged. If you're not doing so, James has a message for you: *it's time you did.*

James makes it very clear that caring for the disadvantaged and those on the margins of society is the responsibility of every Christian. In fact, he pushes his instructions a bit further. Those who don't "visit orphans and widows in their affliction" (ESV) are practicing a false religion. Make no mistake, the "religion" James is referring to isn't the institutional church so many people shy away from these days. In this case, "religion" represents what we believe about God and His Word—in other words, the very faith we say we have. If we don't do our part for those people subject to exploitation, who are on the fringes of the social, economic, and legal landscape, our faith isn't worth much. In fact, as James famously points out later in his letter, a faith that doesn't result in action is worthless. On the flip side, when we do our part—whatever that is—we are in line with God's heart:

> *He defends the cause of the fatherless and the widow, and loves the foreigner residing among you, giving them food and clothing.*
> DEUTERONOMY 10:18

James has a final word for those who desire to practice a "pure and undefiled" (ESV) faith. True faith gets involved in the world but remains free of the corruption and evil of the world. This doesn't happen automatically. We need to act with intelligence and grace, trusting God and giving Him credit rather than getting caught up in our own pride. We need to be "in" the world, but we have to be careful not to get caught up in the world's values.

- Just because the poor have always been around, we have no excuse for ignoring them.

- Don't call yourself a Christian unless you care about the poor.

- Those who do their part in caring for the disadvantaged are in line with God's heart.

- Have a global perspective when you consider those in need, but don't overlook your own community.

- A wise and mature Christian knows how to be *in* the world without being *of* the world.

My brothers and sisters, believers in our glorious Lord Jesus Christ must not show favoritism.

JAMES 2:1

TWELVE

Don't Show Favoritism

Many people believe that getting into heaven is simply a matter of their "good deeds" outweighing the "bad deeds" they have racked up during their lifetime. It is interesting to hear how people categorize the types of conduct that would be included on the two sides of the scale. In the good deeds category, they focus more on the small and minor acts of kindness (because the heroic good deeds, like dying in a fire while saving an infant from the flames, are a rare occurrence). So the good deeds list includes picking up litter that fell out of the wastebasket at the public library, not stepping on a bug, and directing a lost child to the clerk at the grocery store. In contrast, the bad deeds list includes only horrendous and heinous acts, such as murder, armed robbery, and torture of babies. Understandably, the conduct constituting bad deeds are the outrageous behaviors in which very few of us participate. Absent from the bad deeds list are the kinds of acts that seem innocuous to us but are nonetheless offensive to God and reveal a heart that is self-centered.

Fortunately for all of us, God doesn't dispense salvation on the basis of behavior. We couldn't rack up enough good deeds to offset even one minor infraction. God is a holy God, so *any* transgression by us—no matter how seemingly harmless—falls far short of His righteousness. The only good deed that can provide salvation for us is the sacrificial death of the sinless Jesus. And that was His good deed, not ours.

In his letter to followers of Christ, James celebrates their salvation and the fact that God has forgiven their sins. Yet he cautions them to be mindful of their bad deeds. He isn't talking about the obvious ones that make the list (murder, robbery, etc.); instead, he focuses on what otherwise might be obscure and overlooked sins, such as favoritism.

With all of the evil that is rampant in the world, why would James mention something as bland as favoritism? Probably because we don't take it as seriously as we should.

Favoritism, particularly in a church setting (which

appears to be what James was thinking about), occurs when we treat person A better than person B on the basis of criteria that is shallow and self-serving. We may see no offense in that preference as long as we don't treat person B unfairly or poorly. But when Jesus told us to love our neighbors, He intended that we reflect His love to *all* our neighbors, not just the ones who were wealthier or better looking or had more social connections. God doesn't want us to make such distinctions. God certainly doesn't. His salvation is available to everyone. Christ certainly didn't. He spent much of His time with the people whom "respectable" society rejected for one reason or another.

When we show favoritism, it suggests that we attribute more worth and value to one person than another. This attitude is contrary to God's love, and that is why James views it as a sign of whether we actually have God's love in our hearts.

If we truly love God and want to please Him, we need to change the way we think about our attitudes and actions.

> *Let God transform you into a new person by*
> *changing the way you think.*
> ROMANS 12:2 NLT

Even actions and feelings that we might consider to be inoffensive will be displeasing to God if they are not aligned with His heart for humanity. Favoritism is just such an offense. The more we guard against it, the more we will be accurately reflecting the love of God.

. . .For Changing Times

- Love people as God loves them.

- Be on the lookout for people who might be feeling unloved and unlovable. Then surprise them by showing them love.

- If you want to get closer to God, get closer to the people He loves.

- It is easy to love those who are lovable. Allow the Spirit of God to help you love the seemingly unlovable.

- Don't evaluate the sincerity of your faith solely by the people who are your friends.

If you really keep the royal law found in Scripture,
"Love your neighbor as yourself," you are doing right.

JAMES 2:8

THIRTEEN

LOVE YOUR NEIGHBOR

When it comes to opinions and traditions, we all think we're right. It's human nature. Very few of us give ground on issues we care deeply about—especially those that embrace religion or politics—without a fight. The problem is, most of us have a hard time separating the issue from the issuer. In other words, we tend to label people based on their viewpoints. And if we don't like the viewpoint, we don't like the people.

The people in the church James was addressing in his letter had this tendency as well, but their prejudice involved social status rather than political leanings. They favored those who had more money and more influence over those who were poor and carried no influence. James saw this as a big problem, and he told his readers exactly what he thought about their actions, which were at best hypocritical.

A *hypocrite* is someone who says one thing but does another. Christians are often accused of hypocrisy, not because they're necessarily worse than their unbelieving counterparts, but because they often talk about how much God loves the world and then do or say things that directly contradict this message. It's a fair criticism not to be taken lightly. Truth be told, a Christian who says one thing—especially if it's a directive from the Bible—and then does something that contradicts that directive, even if it's something small, is a hypocrite. In case you haven't noticed, the watching world despises Christian hypocrites and isn't shy about making a big deal out of it. However, if you think the world hates hypocrisy, wait until you see how much God hates it, especially when it comes to favoring certain groups of people over another.

There's no question that the people James was addressing were professing Christians. As followers of Christ, they were well aware of the instructions—you could even call them commands—Jesus gave His followers. In fact, Jesus said a lot about what He expected His followers to do; and just in case there was confusion about any of it, Jesus did us all a big favor by summarizing all of the major commands into two simple sentences:

" 'Love the Lord your God with all your heart
and with all your soul and with all your mind.'
This is the first and greatest commandment.
And the second is like it: 'Love your neighbor as
yourself.' All the Law and the Prophets hang on
these two commandments."

MATTHEW 22:37–40

It doesn't get much more basic than this: *love God and love your neighbor.* In these two commands is the governing principle behind every other law, command, and principle in the Bible.

This is the "royal law" James is talking about. It's supreme, kingly, and all encompassing, coming from the heart of God, who is love (see 1 John 4:7–10). Because James puts emphasis on loving "your neighbor," a logical question to ask is, "Who is my neighbor?" You may recall that someone asked Jesus that question, and He answered by telling one of His most famous parables—the story of the good Samaritan (see Luke 10:25–37). In that story is the best definition of *neighbor* you will ever find. Here it is: a neighbor is anyone in need.

It doesn't matter whether your neighbor agrees with

you or whether he or she is rich or poor, someone with influence, or the least significant person in your community. It doesn't matter if your neighbor looks like you or is someone who couldn't be more different than you. And perhaps most crucial of all in these changing times, it doesn't make one bit of difference if your neighbor comes from your religious tradition or is dramatically opposed to your own beliefs. Those of us who call ourselves followers of Christ are called by God Himself to love and accept and care for anyone who has a need, whether it's physical or spiritual or both.

- Carry your opinions loosely, but hold on to truth firmly.

- Rather than taking offense when someone accuses you of hypocrisy, take stock.

- Everyone is a hypocrite at one time or another, because none of us does what we say all of the time.

- The most basic two commands in scripture—love God and love your neighbor—are also the most complex.

- Your neighbors are anyone in need, and it doesn't matter who they are or what they need.

*For whoever keeps the whole law and yet stumbles
at just one point is guilty of breaking all of it.*

JAMES 2:10

FOURTEEN

KEEP ALL OF GOD'S COMMANDS

Keeping God's laws may be a lot tougher than you think. A quick review of the Ten Commandments from Exodus 20:1–17 may give you the wrong impression that it might be possible to slip through a lifetime without a single violation:

COMMANDMENT	DEGREE OF DIFFICULTY
1. No other gods.	Doable.
2. Don't worship carved images.	No problem.
3. Don't use God's name in vain.	I'll use "Aw, shucks" as a swear substitute.

4. Keep the Sabbath holy.	No working on Sunday. Got it.
5. Honor your father and mother.	Send cards on Mother's Day, Father's Day, birthdays, and anniversary.
6. Do not murder.	Slim chance that this would ever happen.
7. Do not commit adultery.	I have no present plans to do so.
8. Do not steal.	Shouldn't be a problem.
9. Do not lie.	I'm sure little white lies are a permissible exception.
10. Do not covet.	No problem as long as I have everything I want.

But a lifetime is a long time. And we aren't as perfect as we think we are. And then along come tough times that change our entire world. Our parents get elderly and cranky, and we lose our patience in dealing with them. (Number 5 violated.) And then finances are very tight, and significant money can be saved by fudging on our tax returns. (Number 9 violated.) And everyone's life seems better and easier than ours. (Number 10 bites the dust.)

And to make matters even more difficult, God takes a broader interpretation of the commandments than a mere *verbatim* reading would indicate. Jesus explained it this way:

> *"You have heard the commandment that says,*
> *'You must not commit adultery.' But I say,*
> *anyone who even looks at a woman with lust has*
> *already committed adultery with her in his heart."*
> MATTHEW 5:27–28 NLT

Here's the reality: you can't keep all of the Ten Commandments all of the time. No one can. That's part of the point of the Ten Commandments. They show the righteousness that God requires but also reveal our inability to live up to that standard.

That's the bad news. But the good news is that Christ paid the penalty for our failure to satisfy the requirements of the Ten Commandments. And if we follow Him, all prior laws and commandments are replaced by a new standard, which Jesus explained this way:

"So now I am giving you a new commandment:
Love each other. Just as I have loved you, you
should love each other. Your love for one another
will prove to the world that you are my disciples."
JOHN 13:34–35 NLT

This new commandment fulfills the Ten Commandments and will produce the results that the Ten Commandments demanded (but could never be attained).

- God gave the Ten Commandments with no expectation that anyone would satisfy them. They show what God requires and that we are incapable of satisfying His standard of righteousness.

- You can't get to God by your good behavior. It isn't good enough.

- Christ's sacrificial death is good enough. Accept the fact that Jesus paid the penalty for your failures, and then you can get to God.

- Rules are an attempt to use outside behavior to make you good inside.

- Love changes you on the inside with the result that your outside behavior improves.

Judgment without mercy will be shown to anyone who has not been merciful. Mercy triumphs over judgment.

JAMES 2:13

FIFTEEN

Mercy Triumphs over Judgment

Two of the biggest themes in the Bible are judgment and mercy. God's judgment is necessary because the world isn't the way it's supposed to be—the way God created it, perfect and free of sin and corruption. Because humankind is in rebellion against God, there has to be a day of reckoning or judgment.

People don't like to hear about God's judgment. It seems so harsh and capricious. We want God to love us without judging us. But that's not the way it works in the real world, is it? We know there are lawbreakers among us—those who inflict harm on others in one way or another—and because we live in a society governed by lawmakers, laws, and courts, we respect the authority of judges and juries who hold lawbreakers accountable. When evil happens, we ordinarily don't call out for the justice system to overlook the wrongdoing. We are eager to see justice served. We want judgment.

Why should it be any different with God? As the creator of the universe and everything in it—including us—He has every right to punish lawbreakers. Only in this case, it's not the civil lawbreakers God is concerned about (God gives this responsibility to the "governing authorities" [Romans 13:1–2]). God is concerned with His perfect moral law.

Part of our discomfort with God as judge is that most of us don't think we have offended God all that much, at least not enough to deserve His judgment and whatever punishment follows. But the truth is that any sin—that is, any deviation from God's perfect standard—offends God, who is perfectly holy (see Isaiah 6:3) and cannot tolerate sinners and the sins they commit.

The other part of our discomfort with God as judge is that we don't understand that God is a perfect judge. Unlike human judges, who sometimes make mistakes, God is always perfect and fair in His judgments (see Psalm 96:10–13). He will never judge or condemn anyone who is not deserving. Still not feeling entirely comfortable with this whole judgment business? Thank goodness—or more appropriately, thank

God—there's more to God's character than judgment. There's also *mercy*, and as far as we sinners are concerned, that makes all the difference in the world.

Mercy is defined as "not getting what you deserve," and that's exactly what God does for us. We deserve judgment because of our offenses, but God gives us mercy. Instead of giving us what we deserve—punishment for our sin— He gives us life, not because we're any good, but because He's so good. In fact, mercy is so much a part of God's character and so important to God, that He expects us to act just like Him in this regard. Because God has shown us great mercy, He wants us to be merciful as well.

Jesus once told a story about a man who was not merciful after he'd been shown great mercy by someone he had offended. To say the least, it didn't go well for the unmerciful man (see Matthew 18:21–35). Jesus said, "Blessed are the merciful, for they shall receive mercy" (Matthew 5:7 ESV).

But how do we show mercy, especially in these changing times? With so much evil and suffering in the world, what can we possibly do that shows mercy to others, especially when circumstances are outside our control? Fortunately, we don't have to look very hard to find the answer. In fact, James pretty much addresses this issue in his letter. When we show favoritism, we are not showing mercy. Even more pointedly, when we fail to show compassion for the poor and the powerless, we are not being merciful. As God says:

> *"Administer true justice; show mercy and*
> *compassion to one another. Do not oppress the*
> *widow or the fatherless, the foreigner or the poor.*
> *Do not plot evil against each other."*
>
> ZECHARIAH 7:9–10

This theme of mercy rather than judgment—or as James puts it, mercy triumphing over judgment—is incredibly important for our own well-being. Are things not going well for you, even in the small stuff of your life? Do you feel as if you are being judged, not just by others, but by God Himself? It's quite possible you are judging others and failing to show them mercy. This is a principle that has no boundaries. It starts with your neighbor, your coworker, even your fellow believer— but it doesn't stop there. The mercy and compassion God shows to us should prompt us to be merciful and compassionate to others. And it should make us want to imitate His justice—which is nothing if not merciful—as we consider the poor and the powerless.

. . .FOR CHANGING TIMES

- We want God to go easy on us when we disobey Him, but we like it when judges throw the book at lawbreakers.

- Even the best of human judges make mistakes, but God makes the right call every time.

- Of all the things we thank God for, His mercy should be at the top of our list.

- Whenever you are tempted to withhold mercy from someone who has wronged you, think about the mercy God has given you.

- Showing mercy to others should have no boundaries.

Faith by itself, if it is not accompanied by action, is dead.

JAMES 2:17

SIXTEEN

FAITH WITHOUT ACTION IS DEAD

Many people have tried to hypothesize a grudge match between two of the Christian stalwarts of the first century. The hype has a lot of appeal. On one side would be the apostle Paul, a guy who wrote more than half of the New Testament books. On the other side would be James, the half brother of Jesus Christ.

Paul would be fighting for the proposition that salvation comes through faith alone. No action is required on our part. He said it this way:

> *Can we boast, then, that we have done anything to be accepted by God? No, because our acquittal is not based on obeying the law. It is based on faith.*

So we are made right with God through faith
and not by obeying the law.

ROMANS 3:27–28 NLT

James, on the other hand, is quick to assert that "good deeds" are involved in the faith process. He is looking for obedience and godly conduct. Here is what he said:

So you see, faith by itself isn't enough. Unless it
produces good deeds, it is dead and useless.

JAMES 2:17 NLT

Are these two saints expressing irreconcilable differences? Actually, no. They share the same theology but are making different points.

When Paul says that faith alone is required for salvation, he is emphasizing that no effort by us earns any part of salvation. Rather, salvation is a free gift from God. Paul is talking about the moment and act of salvation. He is not talking about what happens afterward in the life of a follower of Christ. James would agree with all of this.

On the other hand, the epistle of James was written to people who claimed to be followers of Christ. Given that audience, James didn't spend time talking about the process of salvation. Instead, he was concerned that many of these people were self-deluded because they claimed to be religious follow-ers of Christ but weren't acting like it. For them, he explained that those who claim to love God should show evidence of good works in their lives. He was challenging the sincerity of their faith. Claiming to love God isn't proof that a person really loves Him. The best evidence of an authentic commit-ment to God is whether a person's behavior is consistent with that claim. Paul would agree with all of this.

On this both Paul and James would concur: salvation comes from faith alone. We can do nothing to earn it. Our good deeds are meaningless for purposes of obtaining salva-tion. But once we belong to God and have committed our lives to Him, our good deeds may be an accurate indicator of the sincerity of our faith. Because God told us to love others, we ought to be doing that. If we aren't loving others, and if we aren't even interested in trying, then maybe we aren't as com-mitted to Christ as we claim to be.

This distinction has particular relevance when life turns difficult and events change our circumstances for the worse. In those situations, we are often forced to work harder because any hope for future restoration may be dependent, in part, on our own effort. In these situations, we have to take on a work-hard mentality. But we must never apply that work-hard ethic to our salvation. That's God's responsibility. And after that, our work for Him shouldn't be a chore. It should come from a natural response of appreciation out of our love for God.

- God won't love you more because of your good deeds. Besides, your good deeds probably aren't as impressive to God as they are to you.

- God won't love you less because of your bad deeds. There is nothing that you have done that can't be covered by God's forgiveness.

- Good deeds and bad deeds are irrelevant for salvation. Your faith in Christ is what brings salvation. Your behavioral history has nothing to do with it.

- But once you claim to be a follower of Christ, then it is reasonable to expect that there will be a change in your lifestyle that reflects a transformation in your outlook.

- Don't worry about getting good before you come to God. Come to Him as you are. But expect changes after that. Not because God forces it, but because you'll desire to honor Him by changing the way you live.

You believe that there is one God.
Good! Even the demons believe that—and shudder.

JAMES 2:19

SEVENTEEN

BELIEF IN GOD IS NOT ENOUGH

Everybody believes in something. In fact, we believe in many things, which is good! Without belief, we would never leave our homes.

Belief is foundational for living in the small stuff and the big. Think about your day for a minute. When you get up in the morning and get ready to go to work or school or some appointment, you believe the temperature of the water in your shower won't scald you. You believe your hair dryer (assuming you have enough hair to dry) won't electrocute you. When you sit down to eat breakfast, you believe your food is safe to eat and that some demented food worker hasn't put poison in your oatmeal. You get in your car and drive to your destination, believing the other drivers are going to obey the rules of the road and make it safe for you to drive. On and on it goes.

In this regard, belief is a lot like faith because it involves trust, which ultimately involves the heart more than the head. You may have knowledge of something—for example, you may vaguely know how an airplane works and believe in the principle of aerodynamics—but until you actually *trust* the mechanism and the physics of flying and the skill of the pilot, causing you to commit yourself to board the airplane, you haven't put your faith in the flying experience.

The same principle applies to belief when it comes to God. It's one thing to say you believe in God, that He exists even though you can't see Him. You may even know some of the classic arguments for the existence of God. Good for you! You believe in God with your head, but you haven't yet trusted in God. You haven't committed yourself to Him. Your belief hasn't gone to your heart.

Do you know who else believes in God? According to James, the demons believe in God. Okay, maybe that's a little otherworldly, so let's get down to earth for a couple of examples. How about Adolf Hitler? He believed in God. So did Jeffrey Dahmer. So do a lot of people who aren't mass murderers or serial killers. It's not that hard. As someone once said, it takes more faith to deny God's existence than to believe in

Him. So believing in God's existence isn't such a big deal.

In these changing times, the so-called new atheists have worked hard to discredit God's existence. Don't be fooled—nothing about these atheists is new. Certain people have always tried to disprove God's existence, but theirs is a futile endeavor, because it's impossible to deny God's existence. Do you know why? The reason is simple. When God created humanity, He put His divine imprint in every person (see Genesis 1:26–27). And as if that weren't enough, God put a longing for eternity in every heart as well (see Ecclesiastes 3:11). Even if people deny the facts of God's existence (and there are plenty), they instinctively know that God is real (see Romans 1:19–20).

No, the problem is not that people don't believe in God. The problem is that they believe in God with their heads but deny Him with their hearts. We call this the "no-man's-land" of belief. It's a place where a person believes God exists but lives as if He doesn't. Sadly, many Christians live in this place. They believe in God just enough to get the benefits. The way they figure it, if there's a God, then there's a heaven, which is where they want to go when they die. In the meantime, they want a happy life with good health and plenty of money. Basically, their belief is all about them and not much about God.

True belief, the kind James is talking about here, comes through the head to the heart and leads to a changed life filled with those deeds and "good works" (Ephesians 2:10) that God wants His children to do. Please hear us. We're not saying (and neither is James) that believing in God's existence isn't important. Knowing that God is real and true is essential to knowing God. But believing in God should be coupled with believing God's Word and doing those things God wants us to do.

- True belief comes through the head to the heart and leads to a changed life.

- You don't really believe something until you commit yourself to it.

- There are no true atheists, because every person instinctively knows God exists.

- The belief of many people is self-centered when it should be God-centered.

- People who truly believe in God take Him seriously and do what He says.

You see that a person is considered righteous by what they do and not by faith alone.

JAMES 2:24

EIGHTEEN

YOUR FAITH IS NOT ALONE

God knows whether you belong to Him. There's no fooling Him. Either you do belong to Him or you don't, and He knows with absolute certainty. But how do you know for sure about your *own* salvation? And what about other people? Aside from your affirmations that you love God, is there a way others can know if you are telling the truth?

To get to the heart of this matter, we need to travel back to the first century. Back to the city of Jerusalem on the evening before Christ was crucified. In a second-story room, Jesus is having His last dinner with His disciples. He knows what is going to happen in the next few hours, but they don't. Like a general giving a farewell address to the troops before battle, Jesus is giving a pep talk and vital information to His men—information they'll probably soon forget but hopefully will remember when they need it most.

Among the subjects He covers, Jesus explains that He will be returning to heaven shortly. In His absence, God will send the Holy Spirit—which Christ refers to as "the Comforter"—to earth to indwell Christ's followers. The Holy Spirit's role will be to give spiritual reassurance to everyone who believes in Christ. This is the reason why the Bible refers to our bodies as the "temple of the Holy Spirit"—because it is the place where the Holy Spirit resides.

> *Don't you realize that your body is the temple of the Holy Spirit, who lives in you and was given to you by God?*
>
> 1 CORINTHIANS 6:19 NLT

So, for yourself, God will give you the Holy Spirit in your life to confirm your salvation.

> *For his Spirit joins with our spirit to affirm that we are God's children.*
>
> ROMANS 8:16 NLT

But the reality of your relationship with God should also be readily apparent to the people who know you. Over time they should notice differences in your life that are the result of the Holy Spirit residing in you. The Holy Spirit's influence in your life will produce or enhance characteristics that reflect God's nature. The Bible refers to this influence as the "fruit" of the Holy Spirit.

But the Holy Spirit produces this kind of fruit in our lives: love, joy, peace, patience, kindness, goodness, faithfulness, gentleness, and self-control.
GALATIANS 5:22–23 NLT

With those character qualities growing in your life, your family and friends are bound to notice that something is different about you.

While you become a child of God by your faith alone, that is not a singular event. God will be at work in your life. You will be on a journey of spiritual maturity that broadens your understanding of God as the Holy Spirit gives you an understanding of God's nature. In addition, you will begin to exhibit the fruit of the Spirit in your life. These changes will be noticeable.

While the act of placing your faith in God may be a private matter, the result of your faith produces evidence that makes your faith public. It begins with faith, but a life committed to God translates that faith into loving action.

. . .For Changing Times

- You can't commit your life to God and remain the same. Changes will take place within you, and they'll all be for the better.

- Faith in God leads to God in you.

- Belonging to God comes by faith alone. But with that faith comes the Holy Spirit, and with Him you are never alone.

- The Holy Spirit's role is to make us more like Christ.

- Our lives can be sin filled or Spirit filled. God gives us the free will to decide which way we want it to be.

*Not many of you should become teachers, my fellow believers,
because you know that we who teach will be judged more strictly.*

JAMES 3:1

NINETEEN

THE BURDEN OF TEACHING

The power of words is an awesome thing to behold. A simple phrase has been known to comfort an entire nation, such as Franklin Roosevelt's famous "The only thing we have to fear is fear itself" speech given at his first presidential inauguration in the depths of the Great Depression. At other times, words can ignite a team, such as the historic "Win one for the Gipper" talk Knute Rockne gave to his Notre Dame football players at halftime, motivating them to turn the tables on certain defeat.

But words can also be destructive, causing misunderstandings, inflicting emotional damage, ruining reputations, or worse. Just one example we are seeing in these changing times—when technology connects people in dazzling ways—

is cyberbullying, in which students direct hateful comments to a fellow classmate on a seemingly benign social media platform, sometimes causing great tragedy.

James is very aware of the power of words to both praise and do harm. In this chapter and the three that follow, we're going to look at what he has to say about that small part of the body responsible for words and speeches and unplanned outbursts (not to mention criticism, gossip, and bullying). First, in this chapter we want to focus on a specific group of people who use words more than most people. In some cases they even use words for a living. They're called teachers.

All of us stumble in various ways because of ill-timed or poorly chosen words. All of us have spoken maliciously at times, often without premeditation. As we will see, we are held accountable for our words just as readily as we are held accountable for our actions. But according to James, those who teach—especially those who teach from the Word of God—are held to a higher standard than those who don't teach. That's why he issues this warning: "Not many of you should become teachers."

Teachers are incredibly important people, and good teachers are in high demand. Why? Because they impart information the rest of us need in order to grow in knowledge and skill. In the case of those who specialize in the Bible, the information and the knowledge they teach is vital for what the apostle Paul calls "spiritual wisdom and understanding" (Colossians 1:9 NLT). But unless the words they use to guide others in the faith are rooted in the truth of the Bible, teachers have the potential to lead God's people off the path of right living, something God does not approve of. This is what Paul had in mind when he wrote the following to his protégé, Timothy, who was a teacher just like Paul:

> *Do your best to present yourself to God as one*
> *approved, a worker who does not need to be ashamed*
> *and who correctly handles the word of truth.*
>   2 TIMOTHY 2:15

There's another aspect to teaching the Bible that teachers need to take seriously. It isn't enough to be *correct* in your teaching. You can be accurate in your interpretation and explanation of what the Bible says about this or that. But if the life you are living doesn't demonstrate the fruit of what you are teaching—in other words, if you don't practice what you preach—then the truth you are doing your best to explain will have little impact. In fact, you may even turn people away from the truth because there's no spiritual fruitfulness in your life.

We know teachers have a lot to live up to. That's why James discourages most people from taking on such a burden. However, if you believe God has called and equipped you to teach His Word to others, consider it a privilege and never forget the responsibility you have—with God's help—to explain it correctly and live it fully.

- Whoever said, "Sticks and stones may break my bones but words can never hurt me," didn't know a thing about real life.

- God holds us accountable for our words as much as He holds us accountable for our actions.

- Teaching God's Word should be taken seriously because God takes it seriously.

- Good teaching leads to good learning.

- A fruitful life leads to teaching that bears fruit.

When we put bits into the mouths of horses to make them obey us,
we can turn the whole animal.

JAMES 3:3

TWENTY

SMALL THINGS MAKE
A BIG DIFFERENCE

When times change and life gets rougher, we are often knocked down and set back. A great deal of effort may be required to get back up. It might take quite awhile. Getting back on our feet is an accomplishment, but that would put us back to where we were. We need to move forward, yet sometimes we might not know how.

Whether our setbacks involve our finances, our health, our relationships, or our job, sometimes the distance of our recovery is so great that it is intimidating. We can be in debt so deep that a complete payoff is totally unrealistic. Maybe a relationship seems so broken that there are no open lines of communication—and restoring the relationship can't happen if there is no possibility of discussion. Health challenges can seem to be without hope if the doctor's prognosis is nothing more than a time frame for remaining life expectancy. And if you're looking for work, it is hard to create a job for yourself.

The irony of tough times is that we are forced into circumstances that involve huge problems, and these problems seem disproportionately large for the infinitesimal steps that we can take toward our recovery. The disparity seems so great—and depressing—that we are tempted to abandon any of those small recovery steps that are available to us. But you shouldn't overlook those small steps. Just because they are the only course of action available doesn't mean they aren't the best course of action.

The Bible is filled with illustrations of how a little can produce a lot. On the negative side, the Bible warns against little problems that can become bigger:

- *False teaching:* "A little yeast works through the whole batch of dough" (Galatians 5:9).

- *An uncontrolled tongue:* "A tiny spark can set a great forest on fire" (James 3:5 NLT).

Conversely, the Bible also talks about a little good being multiplied for a great benefit:

- *Faith:* "You don't have enough faith," Jesus told [his disciples]. "I tell you the truth, if you had faith even as small as a mustard seed, you could say to this mountain, 'Move from here to there,' and it would move. Nothing would be impossible" (Matthew 17:20 NLT).

- *Miracles:* "Jesus took the five loaves and two fish, looked up toward heaven, and blessed them. Then, breaking the loaves into pieces, he kept giving the bread to the disciples so they could distribute it to the people. He also divided the fish for everyone to share. They all ate as much as they wanted, and afterward, the disciples picked up twelve baskets of leftover bread and fish. A total of 5,000 men and their families were fed from those loaves!" (Mark 6:41–44 NLT).

If you are trapped by your circumstances and don't know how to start digging out on your way to recovery, put this biblical principal to work in your own life in a positive way. Start with something small and allow God to multiply its effects. Do something. Take some action. Don't worry that it seems small while the problems continue to loom large.

The very fact that you are being proactive will make you feel better about your situation and about yourself. And your perspective will brighten more as you learn to depend on God for your ultimate recovery. Trust that He will provide for all of your needs according to His riches in heaven (see Philippians 4:19).

. . .For Changing Times

- "God helps those who help themselves." That's not a Bible verse, but it sounds like one.

- Are you wondering what a first small step is that you can take in the recovery process? Try prayer.

- Your steps may be small, but your God is big.

- Pray as if everything depends on God, but work as if everything depends on you.

- God may allow you to be in a deep hole so that you are forced to look up to Him.

The tongue is a small part of the body, but it makes great boasts.

TWENTY-ONE

THE POWER OF THE TONGUE

Few things in the natural world are more destructive than fire. From a small spark, the flames from an out-of-control fire can destroy a forest in a matter of days. Raging infernos have been known to devastate an entire neighborhood in just a few hours. The longer fires are left to burn, the bigger they get, yet you can almost always trace their origin to a single source.

It's not suprising that James uses fire as a metaphor for the tongue. After citing two examples of small parts capable of guiding bigger things (a bit in a horse's mouth and a rudder under a ship), he uses an example of something large (a forest) tragically affected by something much smaller (a spark). And with the size differential comes an even greater contrast.

With bits and rudders, the whole idea is to *control* the larger object. But that's not the case with a spark. Once the fire is lit, controlling the result becomes almost impossible. So it is with the tongue.

Nothing in the universe is more powerful or more influential than the human tongue. When used correctly—as a helpful guide, an object of persuasion, or a beautiful descriptor—the tongue is as beautiful as anything the human body has at its disposal. Magnificent words, beautiful speeches, phrases filled with praise and encouragement—all of these come from the tongue and can be enormous helps and inspiration to people. But just as likely, the tongue can produce discouragement and devastation.

An unguarded word—sometimes unintended, sometimes not—can have massively disproportioned effects. Something spoken in anger, an insult slung in retribution, or a lie told carelessly or in spite—these are the sparks that can ignite a raging inferno with disastrous consequences.

James says that the tongue has such great potential for harm because it is full of wickedness. Of course, the wickedness doesn't originate in your mouth. It comes from a place deeper inside of you: your heart. Christ taught that all of our sin originates there:

"For out of the heart come evil thoughts—murder, adultery, sexual immorality, theft, false testimony, slander. These are what defile a person; but eating with unwashed hands does not defile them."

MATTHEW 15:19–20

In these changing times, incivility seems to be on the rise, marked by the way people talk to and about each other. Especially in public discourse, gone is the time when one political candidate spoke well of an opponent. The times when people can have a mutually respectful conversation about controversial subjects at a dinner party are few and far between. Instead of expressing respect for someone who has another opinion, many people show disdain. Rather than honesty, there is deceit. And instead of being humble and self-depreciating, people boast. Where are the manners? Why so much slander? Why aren't people content? All we hear is complaining. And it all comes from the tongue.

James is bothered by the damage being done by the tongue, and so should we be. Here's why. As John MacArthur says, the tongue "is a tattletale that tells on the heart and discloses the real person." The tongue is merely an instrument playing a tune composed in the heart. Our words give us away.

We may not mean to say something hurtful, but there's no denying where those words come from.

Even more than causing hurt, the tongue has the power to cause evil, regardless of whether the words are carefully planned or spoken in the heat of an angry moment. Because of this power, James calls the tongue a "restless evil" (James 3:8), suggesting a wild animal fighting against restraint. And when it does break free, the tongue can destroy in all kinds of ways—morally, socially, economically, and spiritually.

So what do we do? James doesn't offer any specific advice at this point, but we can develop a strategy based on the origin of the tongue's destructive patterns. In other words, to guide what comes from the tongue, we need to guard what's in the heart.

. . .FOR CHANGING TIMES

- We all underestimate the power of the tongue.

- A raging inferno can be brought under control, but not until the damage has already been done.

- One of the most shocking things we could ever hear would be one politician speaking well of another. But wouldn't that be refreshing?

- Civility is lost on people who are deceitful, proud, and discontent.

- Guarding what comes from the tongue begins with guarding what comes from the heart.

With the tongue we praise our Lord and Father, and with it we curse human beings, who have been made in God's likeness.

JAMES 3:9

TWENTY-TWO

ARE YOU PRAISING OR CURSING?

Have you noticed how angry a lot of people are in these changing times? Whether it's a whole panel of people on one of those television news shows yelling over each other, someone at a public meeting getting all worked up, or simply two people arguing over who knows what, it seems as if everyone is upset. And when anger erupts, guess what often follows? Cursing.

Typically when we hear the word *cursing* we think of profanity, obscenities, and taking the Lord's name in vain (otherwise known as blasphemy). By that definition, there's plenty of cursing to go around. We hear it in public places, on television and in the movies, and sometimes in our own homes. When James uses the word *cursing*, he may be referring to that kind of speech, but he also has a much broader view in mind. For James, cursing includes slander, gossip, lies, and other verbal abuse. It's the kind of speech that does more damage to other people than simple "swear words" ever could.

As we said earlier, our speech reveals our heart and our character. We may say we are followers of Jesus, but when we talk about others in demeaning, hurtful, and untrue ways, we are betraying the very faith we claim to have. That's because it's inconceivable that the same mouth could both praise God and curse people.

James uses three examples (see James 3:11–12) to emphasize that using our voice to utter offensive statements is contrary to our new nature as Christians (see 2 Corinthians 5:17):

- an underground spring wouldn't produce both bitter water and freshwater;

- a fig tree wouldn't produce olives, and a grapevine wouldn't produce figs; and

- freshwater can't be drawn from a pond of saltwater.

In effect, James is saying that the faith of someone who blesses God and curses the people God made is utterly worthless. Those are strong words, but James is not alone in his harsh assessment. Here's what Jesus says:

> *"What goes into someone's mouth does not defile them, but what comes out of their mouth, that is what defiles them."*
>
> MATTHEW 15:11

On the flip side, Jesus also says that it's impossible for a good tree to produce bad fruit (see Matthew 7:18). By implication, He's saying that bad fruit (or in this case, bad words) can't come from a good heart. Fortunately, there's an antidote for the curse of cursing: a changed heart and a renewed mind. Paul gives this advice:

> *Therefore, I urge you, brothers and sisters, in view of God's mercy, to offer your bodies as a living sacrifice, holy and pleasing to God—this is your true and proper worship. Do not conform to the pattern of this world, but be transformed by*

the renewing of your mind. Then you will be able
to test and approve what God's will is—his good,
pleasing and perfect will.

ROMANS 12:1–2

Can you imagine how different things would be in these changing times if people started talking to each other in a civil, respectful, loving manner? Maybe we can't expect all people to change their speech, but what if those of us who claim to follow Christ decided to use our tongues exclusively as holy instruments rather than destructive devices? One thing is for sure: people who don't have a personal relationship with God would be much more likely to ask us questions about our faith. As Paul writes:

Let your conversation be always full of grace,
seasoned with salt, so that you may know how to
answer everyone.

COLOSSIANS 4:6

If people aren't asking you about your faith, maybe it's because your words are bitter. Invite God into the details of your conversation so that you may show grace to everyone.

- When we slander, gossip, and lie, we are betraying the very faith we claim to have.

- A mouth that never stops cursing will never start praising God.

- Bad words can't come from a good heart, and good words can't come from a bad heart.

- God wants you to conform to His patterns rather than the world's.

- Graceful conversations stand out in an uncivil world.

Who is wise and understanding among you?
Let them show it by their good life, by deeds done
in the humility that comes from wisdom.

JAMES 3:13

TWENTY-THREE

THE HUMILITY OF WISDOM

What if someone were to come to you and say, "Whatever you ask for, I will give you"? How would you respond? Would you ask to have all your debts paid? To have health for yourself and your loved ones? For all of your relationships to be restored? Before you answer, consider this: what if God were to ask you the same question? Would you answer any differently?

Did you know that God actually made this offer to someone? His name was Solomon, the king of Israel, and God said to him, "Ask for whatever you want me to give you" (1 Kings 3:5). Here's how Solomon answered:

"So give your servant a discerning heart to govern your people and to distinguish between right and wrong."

1 KINGS 3:9

Because Solomon didn't ask for the things most people in his position probably would have asked for—more wealth, health, and power—God gave Solomon what he wanted, and the rest, as they say, is history. Solomon may have stumbled in some areas, but he definitely was a wise man who deftly handled many difficult circumstances and wrote some of the world's most inspiring wisdom literature. In fact, we can thank Solomon for passing on his God-given wisdom so that we could learn and benefit. Among our favorites is this advice from the book of Proverbs:

Trust in the Lord with all your heart and lean not on your own understanding; in all your ways submit to him, and he will make your paths straight.

PROVERBS 3:5–6

This idea of leaning on God for wisdom and understanding is at the heart of the way James characterizes a wise person. "Who is the wise and understanding person?" he asks.

There are two ways to know: the wise and understanding person lives a good life and does good deeds out of a humble heart. That's the summary or the result of what comes from wisdom. But how do we get there? How do we become wise?

It's crucial to recognize that there are two kinds of wisdom: *earthly* (or human) wisdom and *heavenly* (or godly) wisdom. Earthly wisdom relies mainly on knowledge, whereas heavenly wisdom comes from God and governs the application of knowledge and truth to everyday life.

In Solomon's day, wisdom meant living life skillfully and helping others to do the same. James gets even more practical. The indicators of a wise person are the things he has already talked about—showing impartiality to the rich and the poor, expressing faith through good deeds, and learning to control the tongue and use it for good rather than evil. Do these things out of humility, and you will truly live a "good life," one that is wise and pleasing to God.

How do you get to such a place in your life, where your heavenly wisdom is revealed by the kind of life you live? James gave us the prescription earlier in his letter:

If any of you lacks wisdom, you should ask God,
who gives generously to all without finding fault,
and it will be given to you.

JAMES 1:5

Can you imagine what kind of world this would be if more people lived this way? Dare we say, what kind of world would this be if more *Christians* lived this way? Would the world be a better place? Would there be less disease, less financial misery, more social harmony? We can only speculate, but there's one thing we know for sure. If those who claim to follow Christ asked for the wisdom Solomon received and lived the "good life" James is advocating, the people who have only earthly wisdom at their disposal would view Christians much differently than they do now. That's why the apostle Peter advises:

Live such good lives among the pagans that, though
they accuse you of doing wrong, they may see your
good deeds and glorify God on the day he visits us.
1 PETER 2:12

. . .FOR CHANGING TIMES

- Asking God for wisdom is the first step to getting it.

- Leaning on your own understanding makes life a whole lot tougher than it needs to be.

- A wise person lives a good life and does good deeds that come from a good heart.

- There's nothing wrong with knowledge, but knowledge alone won't give you wisdom.

- Those who have heavenly wisdom live in a way that shows they have it.

Such "wisdom" does not come down from heaven but is earthly, unspiritual, demonic. For where you have envy and selfish ambition, there you find disorder and every evil practice.

JAMES 3:15–16

TWENTY-FOUR

THE PROBLEM WITH EARTHLY WISDOM

Not everything in life is black and white. Sometimes there are shades of gray. For example, a lot of people like vanilla ice cream, and others prefer chocolate. But nobody will criticize you (and it doesn't make any difference) if rum raisin is your favorite.

Wisdom, however, is pretty much black and white. That's because wisdom isn't just information or knowledge. It's knowing how to apply that knowledge in the context of God's truth. As James has already pointed out, there are just two kinds of wisdom—earthly and heavenly. One is a faulty and perverted wisdom devised by humanity; the other is exemplary wisdom that comes from God.

Do you want to know where most problems come

from in these changing times? From earthly wisdom. Everything we see around us—the financial uncertainty, the incivility, the great divide between rich and poor, the inhumane way some people treat others—comes from earthly wisdom.

When James calls this wisdom "earthly," he isn't saying that the physical order is evil or that everything humans do is bad. Instead, he is referring to a way of thinking that does not take into account God's involvement in and sovereign rule over all creation. In fact, rather than acknowledging God as the creator of all things and serving Him accordingly, many people in our culture have chosen to serve the things God made. In other words, they've substituted the creation for the Creator. And in doing so, they have chosen earthly wisdom over heavenly wisdom. There's a consequence to this exchange. It's called foolishness. King Solomon, the wisest person who every lived, put it this way:

> *The fear of the Lord is the beginning of*
> *knowledge, but fools despise wisdom and*
> *instruction.*

PROVERBS 1:7

As he often does, James takes this theme a step further and tells us in no uncertain terms just exactly what comes from earthly wisdom: bitter envy and selfish ambition. And for those who think a little envy and ambition can't hurt anything and can even help you climb the ladder of success, James explains what envy and selfish ambition produce: "disorder and every evil practice."

Think about it. What was at the root of the global financial meltdown? What is responsible for the terrible violence and oppression going on in many nations these days? What causes division between races, classes, and sometimes families? You got it: bitter envy and selfish ambition, the hallmarks of earthly wisdom. That's why James can say without any hesitation that this kind of wisdom is also unspiritual and "demonic."

So how do we return to a place where heavenly wisdom characterizes our lives? First, we have to be passionate and intentional about getting the kind of wisdom that comes only from God. As Solomon advises:

> *The beginning of wisdom is this: Get wisdom.*
> *Though it cost all you have, get understanding.*
> PROVERBS 4:7

Second, we need to realize this wisdom is a gift from God (see Proverbs 2:6), and just like any gift, we need to ask for it and receive it. As James has already told us:

If any of you lacks wisdom, you should ask God,
who gives generously to all without finding fault,
and it will be given to you.

JAMES 1:5

In this age of disorder and evil practice, asking for and getting heavenly wisdom is without a doubt the best way to live.

- Most of our problems come from earthly wisdom, while most of our solutions come from heavenly wisdom.

- Heavenly wisdom begins with understanding that God rules over all creation.

- Knowledge begins with the fear of the Lord, and wisdom begins with His instruction.

- Getting wisdom begins with asking God for it.

- If you want God to be involved in the small stuff of your life, ask Him for wisdom.

But the wisdom that comes from heaven is first of all pure; then peace-loving, considerate, submissive, full of mercy and good fruit, impartial and sincere.

JAMES 3:17

TWENTY-FIVE

THE BENEFITS OF HEAVENLY WISDOM

We live in a results-oriented culture because human beings are by nature results oriented. We like to be able to measure progress and achievement. How else do you explain the popularity of baseball, a sport that moves at a snail's pace and is getting slower every year? It's because of the nearly infinite array of statistics compiled on every possible nuance of the game. Baseball fans love to track results.

The same goes for the financial markets, our system of education, weight-loss programs, even church attendance. We love outcomes and results. It's the way we were created, and even though we are in the midst of perhaps the greatest culture shift in history, we still want to know what our efforts will get us.

Given this human propensity for measuring things, it's

not surprising that James follows up his list of what happens when you follow earthly wisdom with an even longer list of results that can be expected when you ask for and access heavenly wisdom. According to James, here's what you will be:

- *Pure.* A heart that is pure is considered holy and undefiled. Christ said, "Blessed are the pure in heart, for they will see God" (Matthew 5:8). On the other hand, "without holiness no one will see the Lord" (Hebrews 12:14).

- *Peace-loving.* In the application of heavenly wisdom, people don't attempt to advance their own selfish agenda. Their humility creates an atmosphere of tranquillity. As Jesus said, "Blessed are the peacemakers, for they will be called children of God" (Matthew 5:9).

- *Considerate.* This is about fairness and courtesy in confrontation: "Opponents must be gently instructed, in the hope that God will grant them repentance leading them to a knowledge of the truth" (2 Timothy 2:25).

- *Submissive.* This characteristic isn't about giving up or giving in, but about understanding the opposite side of an argument. The sake of peace in the community prevails over a personal agenda. A submissive person is teachable and willing to make changes against his or her own preference when the alternative doesn't jeopardize the desired outcome. As Paul advises, "Submit to one another out of reverence for Christ" (Ephesians 5:21).

- *Full of mercy.* A merciful spirit does more than just forgive a wrong that has been suffered. It goes beyond forgiveness to extend additional grace and courtesy to the wrongdoer. Jesus underscored the virtue of mercy when He said, "Blessed are the merciful, for they will be shown mercy" (Matthew 5:7).

- *Full of good fruit.* Of course James would insist that good fruit is the outcome of a life genuinely rooted in God's wisdom. Paul agrees: "But the fruit of the Spirit is love, joy, peace, forbearance, kindness, goodness, faithfulness, gentleness and self-control" (Galatians 5:22–23).

- *Impartial.* This should remind you of James's earlier teaching on impartiality. Heavenly wisdom has no room for favoritism. "My brothers and sisters, believers in our glorious Lord Jesus Christ must not show favoritism" (James 2:1).

- *Sincere.* Hypocrisy has no place in God's paradigm. Godly wisdom is honest and without pretense. As the psalmist David writes, "May integrity and uprightness protect me, because my hope, LORD, is in you" (Psalm 25:21).

If you're looking for a "sure thing" in these changing times, you can't do better than heavenly wisdom and the results it produces. But you can't generate these characteristics on your own power, and certainly not with earthly wisdom. You need heavenly help, something God promises if you ask by faith. Only then will you live rightly and peaceably before God and others.

- While the results of earthly wisdom are disappointing, the effects of heavenly wisdom are amazing.

- Heavenly wisdom is pure and peace loving, leading to a tranquil life.

- Considerate and teachable people are filled with heavenly wisdom.

- Impartial and sincere people live with heavenly wisdom.

- When you ask God for wisdom, ask by faith and then use your faith to seek more wisdom.

When you ask, you do not receive, because you ask with wrong motives, that you may spend what you get on your pleasures.

JAMES 4:3

TWENTY-SIX

THE REASON YOU DON'T HAVE

There are few things in life more frustrating and disappointing than not getting what you ask for. Have you ever put in a request for a specific Christmas or birthday gift and not gotten what you wanted? Can you remember how disappointed you were? Or what about that raise you asked for but never received? Were you frustrated and perhaps even a little resentful?

It's no different with God and the things we ask of Him. As much as we try to keep our chin up, we can't help but feel profound disappointment and, if we're being honest, resentment when we don't get the things we ask Him for. Maybe you've hit a rough patch in life and you haven't received from God the results you've been asking for. Or it could be that someone in your family is suffering and, despite your fervent prayers, isn't seeing any improvement.

If you've ever felt this way, James has some timely advice, but it's not the "There, there, everything is going to be all right" kind of advice we all like to get. James is much more direct and honest. "Do you know why you aren't getting what you asked for?" he says. "Because you stink, that's why!" Okay, that's not exactly what James is saying, but it's close.

Keep in mind that James is writing to an audience of Christians in the first century. And while they are separated from us by nearly 2,000 years, our problems are just like theirs. James's analysis and advice are right on the money.

The reason we don't get what we ask God for is because we are fighting with each other. And let's be clear: James isn't writing about Christians fighting with unbelievers, but Christians quarreling with Christians. And just to make sure we don't try to avoid responsibility by blaming the other guy, James beats us to the punch by laying the blame on us and the desires that battle within us. He then proceeds to identify several struggles that characterize those desires. As you review these, keep your Bible open to James 4:2–3 and notice how each is rooted in the kind of bitter envy and selfish ambition that come from earthly wisdom.

- *We want but we don't have, so we kill to get it.* We all struggle with a strong desire for something. It may be for physical pleasure, material wealth, social status, recognition, prestige, power, or something else. But would we actually kill to get the thing we desire? James doesn't mean we would go so far as to actually commit murder, but we might be guilty of engaging in conduct that is destructive to ourselves and others. Our desire for what we don't have, if not controlled, could lead us to commit sins that leave a trail of dead or injured bodies (figuratively speaking) behind us.

- *We want what others have, so we fight to take it away.* Oftentimes our fights and disputes stem from envy for something we want, something possessed by someone else. Maybe we despise someone who has had an easy life while ours has been tough. Or we might direct resentment toward someone who has the kind of joy and happiness that are missing in our own lives.

- *We want, but we don't ask for it.* Often we are so self-centered that it doesn't even occur to us to ask God for what we want. Perhaps we are so self-deluded that we think we're capable of getting what we desire through our own power and devices. Consequently, we don't bother asking God because we think we can obtain it by ourselves.

- *When we ask, we don't get it.* Sooner or later, we recognize the futility of our own efforts, and in desperation we turn to God. But our prayers go unanswered. Our self-centered instinct tells us that God is intentionally trying to frustrate us. In reality our prayers are being answered, but the answer is no because we are praying with selfish motives. We want something simply because it makes us feel better or enriches us in some tangible way.

If there's something you've been asking for but don't have, look for the wisdom found in God's Word. Check your attitude, examine your motives, humble yourself before God, and ask again. He promises to answer.

- Bitter envy and selfish ambition may not lead you to kill, but they have that potential.

- Envy can take many forms, and none of them are unfamiliar to us.

- Self-sufficient people never ask God for anything, and then they wonder why He doesn't give them what they desire.

- Unanswered prayers are directly related to selfish motives.

- It's futile to pray for something that fulfills our sinful desires.

Therefore, anyone who chooses to be a friend
of the world becomes an enemy of God.

JAMES 4:4

TWENTY-SEVEN

Don't Be God's Enemy

Because God is different from us in so many ways, it's sometimes difficult to identify with Him. God is absolutely perfect, all powerful, and all knowing. By contrast, we are imperfect, weak, and not all that bright. We need to understand how much greater God is than us and how much He deserves our respect. As God Himself says:

> *"My thoughts are not your thoughts,*
> *neither are your ways my ways."*
>
> ISAIAH 55:8

At the same time, just because God is infinitely greater and better than us doesn't mean we should keep Him at arm's length like some unreachable star, never approaching Him with true heartfelt emotion and love. God wants us to draw near to Him so He can offer His divine counsel and comfort. God is not some impersonal force. He is a person with emotions just like ours. He loves us more than we could ever love Him, yet He delights in our love. He is fully committed to us and expects us to be fully committed to Him. Like a groom who loves his bride with deep emotion and care, God loves and cares for us (see Isaiah 54:5). What an amazing thing for us to realize! No matter what our circumstances, no matter where we've come from, no matter what we've done, God loves us with an everlasting and unconditional love.

With God's great love comes another emotion we can all identify with—jealousy (see Exodus 34:14). Just as a husband gets jealous when the wife he loves goes astray and casts her affections elsewhere, God gets jealous when His bride—those He has called out and saved by giving His own Son as a sacrifice—betrays His love. In a word, God hates it when we tarnish our relationship with Him by committing adultery—not with another person, but with the world. In fact, God hates it so much that He views our worldly indiscretions as directing hatred toward Him.

"But I don't hate God!" you may protest. "I just like the

nice things the world has to offer. What's the big deal? After all, didn't God create the world?" If only it were that simple. Yes, God made the world, and He loves the world, but the reality is that the world—with its vast array of human institutions, values, and traditions—is against God. Therefore, when we fall in love with the world, we are going against God, and by implication we become His enemy. Not good!

There aren't many who would deliberately set themselves up as God's enemy. That's a battle you can't win. So how does it happen? How is it that people would put themselves in a position to go against God? In our view, the most common reason is that people think they can have it both ways: they think they can love the world and love God at the same time. Indeed, many people live under the delusion that this is possible, and they wonder why they don't feel God's presence in their lives.

Honestly, we think this is why a growing number of people in these changing times are leaving their faith. They've fallen in love with the world and its value system; and as a result, they have forgotten what it's like to feel God's presence and power. But rather than acknowledging their spiritual adultery and returning to the God who loves them unconditionally, they've chosen to leave God. Often they will put up a flimsy excuse or try to put the blame on God, saying He has left them. But unquestionably the blame lies with the leavers because they are the ones who have left God by becoming friends with the world.

Like the Old Testament prophets, who constantly told God's people to turn back to Him, James wants his audience to wake up and smell the coffee. He's asking them to look into God's Word, see for themselves who they really are, admit they are spiritual adulterers, and then do what the Word says (see James 1:25).

Don't be God's enemy, especially in these changing times when everything in the world—the stock market, real estate, the government, even your relationships—is changing like shifting shadows. More than ever, you need to put your trust in the God who is the same yesterday, today, and forever (see Hebrews 13:8), who is all powerful, all knowing, and all loving. Instead of living according to the desires produced by earthly wisdom, which will ultimately lead you to cheat on God and fall in love with the world, make it your goal to fall in love with God once again as you ask Him for the kind of wisdom only He can give.

- Our awareness of God's majesty helps keep us humble.

- "May the Force be with you" does not refer to God, because God is not an impersonal force.

- God's unconditional love means that He loves us with no strings attached.

- It's impossible for us to love the world and God at the same time.

- We always initiate our separation from God, and only God can bring us back to Him.

But he gives us more grace. That is why Scripture says:
"God opposes the proud but shows favor to the humble."

JAMES 4:6

TWENTY-EIGHT

HUMBLE YOURSELF

If there's one thing, above all others, at the root of the ills of the human race, especially in these changing times, it's pride. Wise King Solomon penned what is undoubtedly the most well-known verse on pride in the Bible, and it speaks volumes about the damage pride can do:

> *Pride goes before destruction, a haughty spirit*
> *before a fall.*
>
> PROVERBS 16:18

Look at that last word: "fall." When we read this verse, we usually think of a setback or someone getting knocked off a pedestal because of pride. But the word *fall* has a much more cosmic meaning when you think about the fact that pride was at the root of Satan's rebellion against God and his banishment from heaven. "I will ascend above the tops of the clouds; I will make myself like the Most High," Satan declared (Isaiah 14:14).

Satan's pride led to his downfall. Before God kicked him out of heaven, he was Lucifer, the chief angelic being. Evidently Satan didn't learn his lesson, because he used the same prideful tactic on Adam and Eve, telling them they would "be like God, knowing good and evil" (Genesis 3:5). Once again, arrogance led to a fall that had cosmic implications. Adam and Eve's fall was our fall; their pride is our pride. As James Montgomery Boice observes, "Nothing lies so much at the heart of the problems of the human race as this prideful desire to take over God's place or, which amounts to the same thing, to pretend that we can do without Him."

This desire to do without God, to rely on earthly rather than heavenly wisdom, is at the root of our proud attitudes in this dazzling digital age. The world is literally at our fingertips. The acceleration of knowledge and the expansion of human achievement continue to reinforce our belief that we can know it all and do it all.

Even some churches and religious organizations have

embraced a prideful attitude as they have built impressive buildings, elaborate campuses, and sophisticated media empires. It may be for the sake of spreading the gospel, but ministers and their ministries are just as susceptible to pride as anyone else. And to what end? To tell people about Jesus? Maybe. But as pride creeps in, neither a minister nor a church is exempt from the fall that follows pride.

In these changing times, we've seen the cracks in these man-made structures and systems built by proud people. We've seen enormous financial institutions crumble to the ground. We've watched in horror as real estate prices have fallen as a result of greedy speculation. And we've witnessed once-thriving ministries struggle as their donations have dwindled. It's easy to blame the economic downturn for all of these ills, but it's possible there's another force at work. James makes it clear that God opposes the proud. Could it be that God has allowed humankind's arrogance to soar, thus resulting in all these falls and failures?

The bad news for proud people is that God opposes them because they stand in opposition to Him. Proud, self-sufficient people have little interest in anything or anyone but themselves. When it comes to money, status, and power, proud people live according to the wisdom of the world rather than

God's wisdom. But it doesn't have to be that way.

Just as surely as God opposes the proud, He gives grace to the humble. Humility gets God's attention, primarily because His Son, Jesus, came to earth as a humble servant rather than as a conquering king in order to show us how to live. Not only does God delight in our humility before Him, but He also asks us to live in harmony and humility with one another, never too proud to associate with "people of low position" (Romans 12:16).

In fact, God offers to forgive us and heal us, both individually and corporately, if we simply humble ourselves before Him. And it starts with us, the people of God:

> *"If my people, who are called by my name, will humble themselves and pray and seek my face and turn from their wicked ways, then I will hear from heaven, and I will forgive their sin and will heal their land."*

> 2 CHRONICLES 7:14

...For Changing Times

- Pride is at the root of everything that's destructive, and earthly wisdom is at the heart of pride.

- When they are apart from God, the greatest desire people have is to be like God and know everything.

- That God opposes the proud should send a shudder into us all.

- When it comes to opposing the proud, God doesn't play favorites.

- Just as surely as pride invites God's wrath, humility invokes His favor.

Submit yourselves, then, to God.
Resist the devil, and he will flee from you.

JAMES 4:7

TWENTY-NINE

SUBMIT TO GOD
AND RESIST THE DEVIL

More than 20 years ago, Bob Dylan wrote a song that captured the attention of millions of music fans. It was called "Gotta Serve Somebody." Never one to shy away from making a point in his music, the mercurial Dylan told a listening world, "Well, it may be the devil or it may be the Lord, but you're gonna have to serve somebody."

A lot of people objected to the black-and-white nature of the song's message, but Dylan hit the nail on the head. We may think we're free to live as we like, do what we want, and submit to whom we choose or to no one at all—but the truth is that everybody operates according to one authority or another. And when you boil it all down, there are only two authorities, just two value systems, and only two kinds of wisdom in this world. There is God's authority, God's value system, and God's wisdom; or there is the devil's authority, the devil's value system, and the devil's wisdom.

Previously James alluded to demons (see 2:19) and demonic powers (see 3:15), but now he goes to the source and names the big guy himself—the devil, Satan, the prince of darkness. He's the one who is ultimately behind all earthly wisdom. And like Bob Dylan, James is telling us we have a choice. We can either serve God or serve the devil. But we gotta serve somebody.

Actually, neither James nor Bob Dylan was the first to bring this up. Joshua, one of the great leaders in the Old Testament and Moses' successor, said these immortal words to God's people:

> *"But if serving the Lord seems undesirable to you, then choose for yourselves this day whom you will serve. . . . But as for me and my household, we will serve the Lord."*

> JOSHUA 24:15

Truth is, if you want to follow heavenly wisdom and order your life around God's value system, you have only one choice: serve God. And you can't serve God unless you first submit to Him.

The Bible has a lot to say about submission, because as human beings, we struggle with the idea. Especially in these changing times, all of us have a tendency to question authority, whether it's a teacher at school, a boss at work, or the people who govern us. It's in our nature to rebel and resist. Instead of submitting to external authorities, we want to be our own teacher, boss, and governing authority. That's what earthly wisdom teaches. But heavenly wisdom shows us another way to live.

The Bible tells us first to "submit to one another out of reverence for Christ" (Ephesians 5:21). Just as Jesus had the attitude of a servant (see Philippians 2:7), we need to submit to and serve others, including our employers (see Titus 2:9) and the governing authorities God has placed over us (see Romans 13:1). Sure, abuses occur in the workplace, and sometimes governments are oppressive, but the Bible doesn't tell us, "Submit only if people are nice to you." As James suggests, we always are to be "peace-loving, considerate, submissive, full of mercy and good fruit, impartial and sincere" (James 3:17).

Ultimately and finally we need to submit to God, who will never abuse us or take advantage of us. He will never exploit or hurt us but will always do what's best for us, in the big stuff as well as the small. Why would our response to His loving care and sovereign rule be anything other than wanting to willingly and consciously serve Him and submit to His authority? Truly humble people will gladly give their allegiance to God, obey His command, and follow His leadership.

Finally, a few words about the devil. Even if we don't serve him, we still have to deal with him. Even if we practice heavenly wisdom, we know that "the whole world is under the control of the evil one" (1 John 5:19). Submitting to God will not insulate us from the attacks of Satan. In fact, the father of lies will be more intent on ensnaring us in sin as we become more serious about our faith. (He doesn't waste his efforts on Christians whose faith is ineffectual and unproductive.) But if we refuse to serve the devil and choose instead to serve the Lord, Satan will flee.

. . .FOR CHANGING TIMES

- You can't serve God and the devil at the same time, so you're always serving one or the other.

- Serving God begins with submitting to Him.

- We humans naturally bristle under authority, but God asks us to submit to it.

- Even more, we need to submit to one another out of reverence for Jesus Christ.

- The greatest leaders are the humblest.

Come near to God and he will come near to you. Wash your hands, you sinners, and purify your hearts, you double-minded.

JAMES 4:8

THIRTY

COME NEAR TO GOD

One of the most troubling characteristics of these changing times is alienation. No, we're not talking about living in a land populated by beings from another planet (although we did feel that way once on a trip to New York City). We're referring to the condition of feeling like an outsider or of being alone or estranged. It's the way you feel when you're in a place where others are unfriendly, indifferent, or even hostile.

Our current culture is a breeding ground for alienation. People who hold differing political or religious ideas rarely communicate, and when they do, their words and attitudes are often filled with hostility. The majority of people living in affluence are largely indifferent to those who are suffering in poverty. Alienation has even infiltrated age differences, as the members of one generation shake their heads at the attitudes and actions of another.

And there's the alienation created by our rapidly changing technology. Rather than bringing people together in meaningful and tangible ways, technology makes it possible for us to send messages in an instant without really communicating. The great irony of our age is that people are ever more connected with very little meaningful connection.

Yet with all of these factors contributing to our increasing disconnection with one another, there's another alienation that is far worse. Above all the others, this disconnect leads to unhappiness, frustration, and unfulfilled living. We're talking, of course, about our alienation from God, something that can happen even to those who claim to know Him personally.

Throughout his letter, James has been directing his comments to those who are disconnected and alienated from God. They say they have faith, but they don't really love their neighbor, they don't pay attention to the poor, and their tongues do a lot of damage. These kinds of Christians may think they have a connection with God, but in fact they don't—at least not in the sense of the kind of intimate, dynamic, and meaningful relationship God wants to have with them.

This connection, in which a person truly experiences God's presence, is the most personal and fulfilling experience any human being can ever have. And it's available to anyone who has put faith in God. Unfortunately, few people of faith experience God's presence at this level. They know about God, but they don't really *know* Him in a way that meets the deepest longings of the heart. But life doesn't have to be this way. You can know God deeply as long as you have a true heartfelt desire to experience His presence in your life. God is always there, but He won't force a close relationship with you. God will come near to you, but only if you first draw near to Him.

A lot of people think they can come near to God by basing their relationship with Him on a series of dos and don'ts. They think God will love them more if they do the right things. But God doesn't work that way. Yes, God is pleased with those good works He has prepared for you to do (see Ephesians 2:10), but doing them won't make God love you any more than He does right now. Much more than your performance, God wants your heart—fully devoted to Him, in complete submission to Him, longing for His presence.

And it's not just any heart God wants, but a pure heart that's turned away from earthly wisdom and tuned into heavenly wisdom. Like King David, who disobeyed God greatly but enjoyed God's presence intimately, we need to ask God to give us pure hearts (see Psalm 51:10). Then, as James advises, we need to wash our hands, which is another way of saying "confess our sins." All who want to experience God's presence need to turn away from their offensive behavior and ask God for forgiveness (see 1 John 1:9). As David wrote:

> *Who may ascend the mountain of the Lord?*
> *Who may stand in his holy place? The one who*
> *has clean hands and a pure heart.*
>
> PSALM 24:3–4

This is how we come near to God. This is how we experience His wonderful presence.

- For human connection with God to be truly meaningful, it must be genuinely personal.

- If you are a fan of social media, use it to build meaningful relationships rather than anonymous connections.

- God is a perfect gentleman. He doesn't force anyone to have a relationship with Him.

- God responds to anyone who wants a deeper relationship with Him.

- It is impossible to develop a pure heart without God's help.

Grieve, mourn and wail.
Change your laughter to mourning and your joy to gloom.

JAMES 4:9

THIRTY-ONE

A TIME FOR MOURNING

Sorrow is underrated in our culture. We don't like to be sorrowful, and we try to avoid sorrow. When sorrow hits us and we truly feel regret for something we did, or when we are grieving because of something that happened to us or someone we love, our goal is to get past it and move forward as soon as possible. Nobody likes to live with sorrow. We would much rather have joy in our lives.

So when James advises us to "grieve, mourn and wail" and change our "laughter to mourning," our natural response is to ask why. Why would anybody want to deliberately stop laughing and start mourning? Isn't laughter the best medicine and the perfect way to deal with our present troubles? Doesn't James himself say in the opening to his letter that we are to "consider it pure joy" when we encounter trials? Yes he does, but the path to that joy comes not through laughter, but through sorrow.

Sorrow is not to be taken lightly, and it should not be ignored. Sometimes you can't control when your sorrow comes. You may be grieving right now because of a loss of some kind. Don't discount the feelings you are experiencing. Rather than resenting your current emotional state, embrace it. Instead of doing your best to move on, appreciate where you are and become aware of the benefits of sorrow and suffering.

Perhaps the greatest upside to sorrow and suffering is that they help us identify with Jesus Christ, who experienced both in great measure (see 1 Peter 4:13). If we have any aspirations to be like Jesus—and that should be our constant goal— we must realize that suffering is essential to our spiritual lives. Even Jesus benefited from His suffering. The Bible says Jesus "learned obedience from what he suffered and, once made perfect, he became the source of eternal salvation for all who obey him" (Hebrews 5:8–9).

The truth is that God used suffering in the life of His Son, and He uses suffering in the lives of His children. And for those of us who are aren't willing to follow Him fully, God often uses suffering to get our attention. C. S. Lewis is often quoted for saying, "God whispers to us in our pleasures, speaks to us in our conscience, but shouts in our pains: it is His megaphone to rouse a deaf world."

If you are suffering, whether from a physical difficulty, a financial crisis, or a relational loss, let your sorrow lead you to hope, knowing that God is using it for your good (see Romans 8:28). When you have the hope in your trials that God is using your sorrow for your own good and to make you more like Jesus, you are on the path to joy. This isn't some kind of temporary happiness. It's not even the kind of joy that makes you laugh. It's a feeling of gratitude that comes from a deep part of your soul, knowing that God cares for you greatly and has never for a moment let you out of His love and care.

Now, there's still this matter of turning our laughter into mourning. Is James saying we need to be sorrowful even when we don't feel like it? In a manner of speaking, yes. The first-century Christians were in a situation similar to ours. They had followed false paths to what they thought would lead them to happiness. They were convinced that material things would cause them to laugh. They thought they could experience joy without helping those who were on the margins of society. What they didn't realize is that their pursuit of happiness along these false pathways not only grieved God but also put their own community at risk. So James is telling them to become aware of their sin, realize their guilt, and take responsibility to change. It's hardly a time to laugh. Just the opposite, it's a time to weep.

In these changing and serious times, many are suffering, but there are also many who need to turn their laughter into mourning. We need a godly sorrow that leads to repentance for those things that grieve the heart of God (see 2 Corinthians 7:10). We need to stop relying on the wisdom of this world and humble ourselves before God. Only then will God restore our joy.

. . .For Changing Times

- The path to joy often comes through sorrow rather than laughter.

- A wise person appreciates the benefits of sorrow and suffering.

- Know the difference between the sorrow that comes from your own actions and the sorrow that comes from the Lord.

- God will use all of your suffering and sorrow, regardless of the source, for your own good.

- There is a time to laugh and a time to weep. We need to ask God for the wisdom to engage in each.

But you—who are you to judge your neighbor?

JAMES 4:12

THIRTY-TWO

WHO ARE YOU TO JUDGE?

When it comes to criticizing and finding fault, Christians are very skilled. In fact, some of us consider it a spiritual gift to find and criticize the shortcomings of others. Certainly people in the "world"—those looking at Christians from the outside—are aware of this tendency. Christians in general and some Christian leaders in particular have a reputation for casting judgment on the sins of the culture, and the culture doesn't like it one bit. They want "self-righteous Christians" to keep their morality to themselves and stop judging.

James has some harsh words for this kind of judgmental attitude, but it's not our judgment of outsiders that bothers him. James tells us:

Do not slander one another.

James 4:11

In that simple phrase, there are two important distinctions to unpack. Let's take them in reverse order:

- *One another* could be interpreted universally, but James has a narrower focus, namely, people within the Church. He probably means, "Don't slander other believers."
- *Slander* has a harsh tone to it. While the Bible often condemns gossip, James is talking about something much more serious and sinister. *Slander* involves making intentionally false statements about people for the express purpose of damaging their reputation.

The Bible repeatedly condemns slander. In fact, the Old Testament deals with slander against God or another person more than any other transgression. And the New Testament characterizes slander as despicable in God's sight, such as when Jesus said:

*"Out of the heart come evil thoughts—murder,
adultery, sexual immorality, theft, false testimony,
slander. These are what defile a person."*

MATTHEW 15:19–20

So who were the people in the first century slandering?
According to Bible scholars, it's likely some Christians were
questioning the faith of other Christians based on inconsequen-
tial issues, and this produced unbridled slander in the community. We can identify with this today. Christians judging other
Christians on matters that are not essential to our faith is rampant, in particular when it comes to politics. Those on the right
think liberals are loony, and those on the left think conservatives
are stupid. And each side has a tendency to question the faith of
the other. According to James, this is more than name calling;
it's slander, it's judging, and it's wrong.

A judgmental attitude disrespects God directly. God
alone is our judge. Who else can know the condition of a person's heart? When we judge others, we proudly elevate ourselves and usurp God's authority.

So what should you do if a fellow believer slanders
you? Should you let it go and leave it to God? Although he
doesn't refer to it in this letter, James would heartily endorse

the biblical process for dealing with a difficult situation. Here is how Jesus explained it:

> *"If your brother or sister sins, go and point out*
> *their fault, just between the two of you. If they*
> *listen to you, you have won them over. But if they*
> *will not listen, take one or two others along, so*
> *that 'every matter may be established by the*
> *testimony of two or three witnesses.' If they still*
> *refuse to listen, tell it to the church; and if they*
> *refuse to listen even to the church, treat them as*
> *you would a pagan or a tax collector."*
>
> MATTHEW 18:15–17

Notice that the procedure is consistent with James's teaching in that it keeps the dispute as private as possible at the beginning. The negative repercussions are kept on a need-to-know basis as long as possible, in the hope that the problem can be dealt with privately before it is made public.

If you think keeping all of this straight is a bit complicated, you're right. But it's incredibly important, because the reputation of Christians and the Church before a watching world—not to mention God Himself—depends on it.

- Even more than hypocrisy, the judgmental attitudes of Christians are troublesome to people in the world.

- Gossip is bad enough, but slander is far worse because it is always intentional.

- When the Bible repeatedly condemns something, we need to repeatedly pay attention.

- When Christians judge one another on nonessential matters, they drag God into the gutter.

- You don't necessarily have to be passive when someone else slanders you, but you do need to be wise in the way you respond.

Now listen, you who say, "Today or tomorrow we will go to this or that city, spend a year there, carry on business and make money." Why, you do not even know what will happen tomorrow.

JAMES 4:13–14

THIRTY-THREE

NOBODY KNOWS WHAT TOMORROW WILL BRING

Anybody who thinks the Bible speaks out against money or that Christianity opposes capitalism doesn't know the Bible and true Christian belief very well. Typically, those people focus on a verse such as, "For the love of money is the root of all kinds of evil" (1 Timothy 6:10 NLT), or the words of Jesus telling us that we can't serve both God and money (see Matthew 6:24), and then conclude that a person can't be a Christian—or at least a very good one—and make a lot of money.

On the surface, the phrase "You do not even know what will happen tomorrow" would seem to reinforce the belief that God doesn't want you to plan ahead and get rich. Well, we're here to tell you that nothing could be further from the truth. God isn't pleased with those who don't take responsibility for themselves (see Proverbs 19:24), and the Bible condemns those who don't like to work (see Proverbs 19:15).

By contrast, God is honored when you do well with what He has entrusted to you (see Matthew 25:14–30). The problem with money is not money itself. The problem with money is when it becomes the object of our affections and the priority of our lives. When we think we know what tomorrow will bring—or even worse, that we can control what happens tomorrow—that's when God steps in and warns us to quit focusing on the future.

Truth is, most of us have lived long enough to know that much of what happens in our lives is outside our control. If we are being completely honest with ourselves, we will acknowledge that the trials and tragedies we experience force us to admit that we don't know what tomorrow will bring, and we certainly aren't capable of controlling our circumstances, in the big, as well as the small, stuff. Unfortunately, the wisdom of the world tells us we can be self-sufficient, prompting us to arrogantly speak and act as if the future belongs to us. So we expend inordinate time and resources *working* for the future. Or, in the absence of having enough money and security, we spend a lot of time *worrying* about the future. Both extremes about the future—confidence on one hand and worry on the other—need to disappear so we can follow what Jesus says:

> *"Therefore I tell you, do not worry about your life, what you will eat or drink; or about your body, what you will wear. Is not life more than food, and the body more than clothes? Look at the birds of the air; they do not sow or reap or store away in barns, and yet your heavenly Father feeds them. Are you not much more valuable than they? Can any one of you by worrying add a single hour to your life?"*
>
> MATTHEW 6:25–27

Again, it's important to note that the Bible doesn't condemn wealth or wise planning. What it does condemn—and what James is telling his audience—is that we need to stop believing that money can bring us security. If God has gifted you with material wealth, be grateful and never forget where your ability comes from. Never let your money and wealth define you. Remind yourself daily what Jesus said about material things:

"Watch out! Be on your guard against all kinds of greed;
life does not consist in an abundance of possessions."
LUKE 12:15

On the other hand, if you are struggling financially, and you only wish you could be in a position to make more money and plan for the future, don't fall into the temptation of worrying so much about what tomorrow will bring that you lose sight of what God is doing for you today. And for all of us, our first priority should be God and His purposes for us:

"So do not worry, saying, 'What shall we eat?' or
'What shall we drink?' or 'What shall we wear?'
For the pagans run after all these things, and
your heavenly Father knows that you need them.
But seek first his kingdom and his righteousness,
and all these things will be given to you as well."
MATTHEW 6:31–33

. . .For Changing Times

- Money is neutral, but our attitude toward money is not.

- When we focus too much on the future, we run the risk of assuming we can control it.

- When it comes to the future, there are two extremes to avoid—working too hard and worrying too much.

- When we stop believing that money can bring us security, we start depending on God for the future.

- God is more concerned for our spiritual health than our financial well-being.

Instead, you ought to say, "If it is the Lord's will, we will live and do this or that."

JAMES 4:15

THIRTY-FOUR

DOING GOD'S WILL

Wanting to be the center of attention is in the basic nature of men and women. Why do you think people want to act, run for public office, and participate in sports? Sure, there are those purists who are dedicated to the art of acting, the beauty of athletics, and the service of politics. But most people who engage in such activities are after one thing and one thing only: applause. Whether performers, politicians, or athletes, they are hooked on the rush of recognition. It's all about them.

Of course, the self-esteem movement so prevalent today has only fueled this kind of over-the-top self-centeredness. Children are told from an early age they can do anything they set their minds to. "If you believe it, you can achieve it" is the mantra of our culture, not to mention the prosperity gospel televangelists. Now, we're all for a healthy self-image, but in these changing times, we've taken the concept too far, to the extent that most people are way too impressed with themselves. With so much hot air contained in our overinflated egos, it's no wonder we have pushed God to the margins of our lives.

Contrast these current attitudes with the perspective of the psalmist David, who was a skilled politician, a great commander, and a gifted artist (and let's not forget that as a boy he killed a giant with a stone). When comparing his place in the universe with that of the creator of the universe, here's what he said:

> *What are mere mortals that you should think*
> *about them, human beings that you should care*
> *for them?*

PSALM 8:4 NLT

Now there's some perspective! We can learn from David that our life isn't all that significant when compared to the vastness and eternal significance of God. And we can learn from James that our life is like a "mist" (4:14)—insubstantial and transitory. Whether by illness, accidental death, or the return of Christ, our life could vanish like the mist at any time. Knowing this reality shouldn't depress us. Rather, it should drive us to seek the will of God, who knows us intimately, including the length of our days. Instead of saying, "Here's what I'm going to do," or "This is who I am going to become," we ought to be asking, "What does God want me to do?" and "Who does God want me to be?"

That's the point James is making here. We need to stop our boasting and suppress our arrogant attitudes. God is in charge, not us. If we have put our faith in Him—both for eternity and for now—we should make it our business to find out what He wants for us. In other words, we need to do our best to discover God's will for our lives. Each day of your life is filled with choices and decisions. Some decisions you make automatically (like brushing your teeth), while others take more time and thought (like starting a business). God isn't concerned with the kind of toothpaste you use, but He does care about your new business. He cares about each decision you make to establish your business and build it into a success. God wants your everyday decisions to line up with His everyday will. You get to decide, but God wants you to focus on Him each step of the way. Here are three things you can do to keep your decisions in the context of God's will:

1. *Commit to do the will of God.* Trusting God for your future—whether that future is tomorrow or ten years from now—begins with trusting God now. And you don't have to wait long for the pay-off. Once you have committed to do God's will, God will show you what to do.

2. *See things from God's perspective.* When you insist on doing God's will from *your* perspective, your main concern is *doing.* You get caught up in your own performance. By contrast, when you do things from *His* perspective, you are more concerned about *being.* God wants you to do stuff for Him, but He's more interested in the kind of person you are becoming.

3. *Let God work in you.* The final thing God wants you to know is that you don't have to do His work by yourself. God has promised to help you.

For it is God who works in you to will and to act in order to fulfill his good purpose.
PHILIPPIANS 2:13

- There isn't enough room in our lives for a big ego and a big God. If you have a big ego, you get a small God.

- If you keep your ego in check, you give God room to work.

- People with a healthy self-image know how insignificant they are compared to God.

- God wants your everyday decisions to line up with His everyday will.

- Trusting God for the big stuff in your future begins with trusting God in the small stuff right now.

- God is more concerned with the person you are becoming than the things you are accomplishing.

*Now listen, you rich people, weep and wail
because of the misery that is coming on you.*

JAMES 5:1

THIRTY-FIVE

The Perverted Power of Wealth

Our culture has an obsession with wealth. Even in these changing times, when the fortunes of many have been lost, the public remains transfixed by money and the people who have it.

In light of this cult of excessive wealth that surrounds us, it would be easy to read a verse like James 5:1 and conclude, "Well, that applies to the super-rich, not to me. I'm just barely getting by!" Truth is, the verse does apply to us, at least those of us who live in the affluence of the West. Every single verse in this opening section of James 5 applies to us, more specifically to those of us who believe our troubles will disappear if we only have enough money. That's why Paul wrote to a young pastor:

> *Those who want to get rich fall into temptation*
> *and a trap and into many foolish and harmful*
> *desires that plunge people into ruin and*
> *destruction. For the love of money is a root of all*
> *kinds of evil. Some people, eager for money, have*
> *wandered from the faith and pierced themselves*
> *with many griefs.*
>
> 1 TIMOTHY 6:9–10

Notice it's not money itself but the *love* of money that is the root of all kinds of evil. That's the point James is making in his letter. It's a point we need to pay attention to. Whether you have a lot or you're struggling to stay afloat, here are some principles that provide perspective and guidance:

1. *Storing up treasure on earth is futile.* As many of us know, prosperity can be transitory. It comes and goes. So if we are depending on ourselves and earthly wisdom rather than on God and His wisdom, we could be tempted to hoard money and possessions when we have them. James isn't the only one who condemns this practice. Read what Jesus says:

"Do not store up for yourselves treasures on earth, where moths and vermin destroy, and where thieves break in and steal. But store up for yourselves treasures in heaven, where moths and vermin do not destroy, and where thieves do not break in and steal. For where your treasure is, there your heart will be also."

MATTHEW 6:19–21

It all comes down to the heart. That's where the "real us" is found. The heart is the wellspring of attitudes that eventually turn into action. Instead of hoarding, we need to be giving. Rather than holding on to what we have because we're afraid of losing it, we need to trust God to provide what we need so He can bless others with it.

And God will generously provide all you need. Then you will always have everything you need and plenty left over to share with others.

2 CORINTHIANS 9:8 NLT

2. *Building wealth at the expense of others is wrong.*
Lest you think this applies only to business own-
ers, we all need to take this warning personally. In
whatever way God enables us, no matter how
small the amount, we need to help those at the
margins of society, exemplified by the widows and
orphans James has already mentioned. Not only is
this our responsibility, but it is also a sign of true
faith (see James 1:27).

If we follow these guidelines for "riches"—basically
anything we have above what we need to live—then we will be
able to stand before God and hear Him say:

> *"Well done, good and faithful servant! You have
> been faithful with a few things; I will put you in
> charge of many things. Come and share your
> master's happiness!"*
>
> MATTHEW 25:21

- Often the people who don't have enough money are tempted the most by it.

- If you want to discover a person's heart, find out where his or her treasure is buried.

- To cultivate a generous heart, we must first understand that we serve a generous God.

- God always gives us a heart of generosity so that we can be generous to others.

- The sweetest words any person will hear when he or she stands before God will be, "Well done, good and faithful servant!"

Be patient, then, brothers and sisters, until the Lord's coming.

JAMES 5:7

THIRTY-SIX

Be Patient until the Lord Comes

Setting a date for the end of the world has become something of a cottage industry, especially in these changing times when there's so much uncertainty in the world. Religious doomsayers like to forecast the "day of the Lord." They love to talk about judgment and fire and brimstone. Nasty stuff.

The nonreligious prognosticators tend to focus on calamities brought about by man's treatment of the environment, a substantial percentage of the earth's population being wiped out by a nuclear holocaust, or starvation due to overpopulation (take your pick).

Don't be distracted by these extreme approaches to an event that is indeed coming someday. Some people may not believe it, others may make fun of it, and still others may set a specific date for it, but don't you be fooled by any of it. Be wise and watching for the coming of the Lord. We have no idea when it's going to happen—nobody does—so we need to be prepared at all times (see Matthew 24:42–44).

How can we be so sure the Lord is coming? What if this life is all there is? That's certainly a possibility, but it isn't likely. The "evidence" for the return of Christ and eternal life—something the theologian N. T. Wright calls "life after life"—is pretty strong. Here are three compelling reasons:

- *The Bible tells us the day of the Lord is coming (see 1 Thessalonians 4:13–18).* We don't have the space to make a case for the reliability of the Bible, but here's something to think about. In the Bible there are approximately 2,500 prophecies. To date 2,000 of these have been fulfilled to the letter. What do you think the odds are that the remaining 500 will be fulfilled to the letter? Pretty darn good; in fact, better than good. It's an impossibility that the Bible would be wrong in any of them, including the prophecies concerning the end of the present age and the return of Jesus Christ.

- *Jesus told us He is coming back (see John 14:1–4).* If Jesus is who He says He is—the Son of God, equal to God in every way—then we can take Him at His word.

- *We all have an internal "sense" that life is eternal (see Ecclesiastes 3:11).* Some people may try to deny it, but inside each human being is an awareness that life does not end when this life on earth is over. The reason for this internal barometer is simple: God put it there.

So, if the Lord is coming, we need to be ready, and we also need to be patient. To give us a picture of what this means, James uses the example of a farmer's patience for his crops. In the eastern Mediterranean region, it requires two seasons of rain to mature a crop. Farmers have to wait through both the fall and spring rains. This requires double patience, but the farmer has double confidence that the crop will reach the point of harvest. The same goes for us as we wait for the Lord. We have to be doubly patient, but we have double the surety that the spiritual harvest will come.

Our hope in Christ and His return is not a wishing

hope, but a hope based on the promises of the Bible and the living God. If God is real, so is His promise to return. If the Bible is God's Word, it can be trusted. Someday our patience and our faith will be rewarded.

> *Now faith is confidence in what we hope for and assurance about what we do not see.*
>
> HEBREWS 11:1

- Taking an extreme approach to the end of the world distracts us from the reality that it is going to happen.

- The evidence for the return of Christ is without dispute, but the date for His return is unknown.

- Wise people don't obsess over the return of Christ. They simply watch diligently and wait patiently.

- God would never ask us to watch and wait for something that isn't going to happen.

- The beauty of true faith is that it inspires confidence and gives hope.

Don't grumble against one another,
brothers and sisters, or you will be judged.

JAMES 5:9

THIRTY-SEVEN

Stop Your Grumbling

Being an optimist isn't easy these days. Few are the people who reach into a box of manure convinced there's a pony in there somewhere. Life in these changing times is handing out a lot of lemons, and you don't see many lemonade stands (there used to be more, but a lot of them are now in foreclosure).

What about you? Are you doing your best to have a positive outlook on life, or have you had it bad for so long that your optimism is at an all-time low? And even if you're doing okay financially, are you feeling a little guilty that other people are hurting, especially those in third-world countries where there is extreme poverty, disease, and oppression? Are you frustrated that a growing number of people in our culture are blaming God for these expressions of human suffering, making Him responsible for the world's problems? Maybe you have your own moments of doubt about the way things are. Perhaps you are asking why a good and loving God would allow so much misery in the world.

Feeling bad about the way things are is natural. In fact, if you were perfectly happy and more or less oblivious to all the problems in the world, there would be reason to question your capacity for human empathy. We need to feel the hurt of others and, when at all possible, bear one another's burdens. The truth of the matter is that the whole world is groaning because things aren't the way they are supposed to be (see Romans 8:22). Not only that, but those who have put their faith in God are groaning because of their longing for a time when there will be no more crying or pain or dying (see Romans 8:23; Revelation 21:4).

God hears our groans, and He understands (see Exodus 2:23). He's asking us to be patient even as He is being patient, for one simple reason: God is waiting to make things right in the world so that more people have an opportunity to turn to Him. You see, when people blame God for the world's ills and criticize Him for not putting an end to human suffering, moral decay, and environmental destruction, they need to understand what they're asking for. God will do all of that someday—in fact, He could put the world back in order right now! But to do that, He would need to deal, once and for all, with the source of human sin and misery, which is *us*.

Joni Eareckson Tada, who has lived for 40 years as a quadriplegic and has suffered more than most of us will every know, puts it this way:

> *The rule of thumb is that we experience much suffering because we live in a fallen world, and it is groaning under the weight of a heavy curse. If God being good means He has to get rid of sin, it means He would have to get rid of sinners. God is a God of great generosity and great mercy, so He is keeping the execution of suffering. He's not closing the curtain on suffering until there is more time to gather more people into the fold of Christ's fellowship.*[1]

So what should our attitude be as we live responsibly and effectively in these changing times? On the negative side, we need to stop our grumbling, especially to one another. Sometimes the most pessimistic people in the world are

Christians. This shouldn't be! We may occasionally be frustrated, but we should never turn our frustrations on each other. Not only does our complaining have a negative effect on those around us, but it also makes us susceptible to God's judgment (see Matthew 7:1).

On the positive side, we need to demonstrate a spirit of generosity and patience, not denying that life is filled with trials, but acknowledging that God is being generous and patient with us, wanting as many people as possible to turn to Him before it's too late.

The Lord is not slow in keeping his promise, as some understand slowness. Instead he is patient with you, not wanting anyone to perish, but everyone to come to repentance. But the day of the Lord will come like a thief. The heavens will disappear with a roar; the elements will be destroyed by fire, and the earth and everything done in it will be laid bare.

2 PETER 3:9–10

. . .FOR CHANGING TIMES

- God never minds our doubts and questions about the way He works in the world.

- Whenever you feel the earth groaning, remind yourself that things aren't the way God wants them to be.

- The only reason God is waiting to make things right in the world is because He wants more people to turn to Him.

- God isn't the source of human suffering and misery—humans are.

- A spirit of generosity and patience in these changing times acknowledges that God is being generous and patient with us.

We count as blessed those who have persevered.

JAMES 5:11

THIRTY-EIGHT

THE REWARDS OF PERSEVERANCE

For the longest time, people have done their best to "market" the Christian faith like it's a prize you get for winning a game show. "God loves you and has a wonderful plan for your life" goes one popular pitch. All you have to do is say yes to God, and the rest of your life will be wonderful beyond your wildest dreams. Other approaches treat God like a slot machine. Got financial troubles? Give God some money and you'll get more back.

It's tempting to cast the Christian faith in a positive light. We tend to like the promise of eternal life in heaven, complete with new bodies and mansions on streets of gold, so that's what we think about. When people ask us how we're doing, we naturally respond that things are great (even if they aren't). And while heaven is real and God blesses us far beyond what we deserve, the stark reality is that a life with God also holds many troubles, trials, setbacks, and pain, and it takes perseverance to get through it all.

When we hear the word *perseverance*, we typically think about it in terms of enduring a trial or a time of difficulty. That's close to the meaning—James writes of "patience in the face of suffering" (5:10)—but there's more to it. For the Christian, perseverance isn't an end in itself, but a means to an end. We can endure suffering because we know what will happen in the end. We know who wins the battle. We are confident this often-difficult life will have a glorious end.

When we are patient and we persevere in the face of suffering, we are like a pregnant woman who endures the pain of labor in order to experience the joy of childbirth. We're like the student who prepares for final exams, willing to go through the anguish of studying for the payoff of a good grade or a degree. Life may be a challenge now, but we can endure difficulties because we know a better day is coming.

When you think of suffering in the Bible, your thoughts might go directly to Job, a man who knew a thing or two about the subject. Most people think the book of Job is just about suffering, and unquestionably there's plenty of that going on. But even more than suffering, Job's story is about faith, in particular the faith of someone who was very much like us. Job complained to God, questioned God, and was tempted to give up. In the end, Job persevered because he believed God. He never gave up his faith even though God allowed Satan to test him by intervening in the circumstances of his life, resulting in a series of tragedies.

Job's patience in the face of suffering was demonstrated in his refusal to "curse God and die" (something his wife recommended in Job 2:9). He revealed a perspective on life that was the secret to his endurance of such tragedy. This perspective enabled him to worship God in the midst of adversity with the same intensity and reverence he had during times of prosperity. Job asked his wife, "Shall we accept good from God, and not trouble?" (Job 2:10).

The lesson from Job is simply profound and profoundly simple. It's easy to trust God with the overseeing of our lives when we are enjoying the ride, but we should also trust Him when the going gets hard. Even when it gets *very* hard. And since God brought Job through those trials and restored his prosperity (something that may not happen to everyone), shouldn't we also have the patience to endure, allowing God to work through the difficult circumstances of our lives to accomplish His will for us?

Are you facing a series of setbacks in these changing times? Does it feel as if Satan is tampering with your circumstances? Take heart and believe that God is faithful. He may not restore what you have lost. You may suffer even more. But God will never abandon you in this life, and He has promised an irrevocable guarantee in the next. You can run the race of your life of faith with endurance, because what you are experiencing now is nothing compared to what God has promised for you.

I consider that our present sufferings are not worth comparing with the glory that will be revealed in us.

ROMANS 8:18

- Christianity isn't a commodity to be marketed but a relationship to be appropriated.

- That a life with God is difficult shouldn't surprise us, but neither should it deter us.

- The key to perseverance is more about expectation than endurance.

- As Job said (1:21), "The Lord gave and the Lord has taken away; may the name of the Lord be praised."

- There may not be a reward at the end of your perseverance, but there is a promise.

Above all, my brothers and sisters, do not swear—
not by heaven or by earth or by anything else.
All you need to say is a simple "Yes" or "No."

JAMES 5:12

THIRTY-NINE

LET YOUR WORD BE YOUR BOND

There's a lot of swearing going on these days, and we're not just talking about profanity. The use of the Lord's name in vain (a big no-no in God's eyes, by the way—see Exodus 20:7) is bad enough, but a lot of people are engaged in another kind of swearing, and it's something we all need to guard against.

In these changing times when both public and private conversations between people are laced with incivility, rancor, and general nastiness, one of the core values of interpersonal communication has disappeared. We're talking about *trust*. When two people talk, when a speaker addresses an audience, or when family members communicate, a mutual bond of trust must exist, or the message falls on deaf ears. And it's hard to maintain trust when one person is judging the other and questions his or her integrity. That's exactly what's going on in all kinds of public and private conversations these days.

When trust is lost, many people go to the next level of discourse in order to convince the other side that they have a valid point, and here's where the swearing comes in. When we lose trust, rather than taking time to earn it back, we simply say, "I swear to God that this is true," or "So help me God, what I'm saying is true." We may even hold up our right hand as a symbolic gesture, like a witness does in court when being "sworn" in. If we add this bit of swearing to our statements, we somehow think our opponent (which is anybody who doesn't agree with us) will have no choice but to trust us. There's only one problem with this scenario: God condemns it.

The point of James saying, "Let your 'yes' be yes, and your 'no' be no" (5:12 ESV), is that we should avoid invoking the name of God to bolster the truthfulness of our statements. In everything we say, there should be an element of integrity and trust so that our word is good enough. If our speech is trustworthy, we don't need to swear our truthfulness. It's unnecessary, and worse, it's offensive to God. Here's what Jesus has to say:

"But I tell you, do not swear an oath at all: either by heaven, for it is God's throne; or by the earth, for it is his footstool; or by Jerusalem, for it is the city of the Great King. All you need to say is simply 'Yes' or 'No'."

MATTHEW 5:34–35, 37

. . .FOR CHANGING TIMES

- Your speech says a lot about your character.

- It takes a long time to build trust but just a moment to destroy it.

- God's name should never be used as an expression.

- If you feel the need to bolster your truthfulness in any way, work on the way you handle the truth.

- Let your word be your bond, and then leave it at that.

And the prayer offered in faith will make the sick person well; the Lord will raise them up. If they have sinned, they will be forgiven.

JAMES 5:15

FORTY

Pray for Healing

Recently we talked with a man in his 60s who is being treated for throat cancer. "Cancer is everywhere," he intoned, emotion filling his voice, which was raspy from the radiation treatments he was receiving. We were hardly in a position to argue. Between the two of us, we can count no fewer than eight people we know personally—from a four-year-old child to three professors at the same Christian college—who are currently battling this pervasive sickness.

No doubt your experience is similar. You know people who are valiantly fighting diseases and conditions that have thrown them for a loop. Perhaps you are in a struggle of your own, whether it's sickness or a setback or trouble of any kind. These are difficult days, and matters both big and small are troubling many of us—dare we say *most* of us. And people of faith don't seem to be exempt. In fact, it seems that Christians are being confronted with more than their fair share of suffering, especially when you look at the situation from a global perspective.

We can't explain why this is the case, other than to say once again that God never promises His children a free pass on suffering. If anything, He promises just the opposite. "In this world, you will have trouble," Jesus warns us (see John 16:33). You don't sign up for a life of faith in the one true God in order to have a happy, pain-free existence. It was true in the first century, and it's still true today.

So why do you believe? What advantage do you have over someone who doesn't believe? Besides the eternal benefit, which we accept by faith, we can think of at least one advantage, and it's pretty big. God may not keep you *from* suffering and sickness, but He promises to get you *through* any kind of trouble life throws at you (see 1 Corinthians 10:13), as long as you invite God into the details of your circumstances— whether good or bad—through prayer.

> *Is anyone among you in trouble? Let them pray.*
> *Is anyone happy? Let them sing songs of praise.*
> JAMES 5:13

But what about sickness? How do we pray for someone who has cancer? What kind of faith is required for healing? It's a huge question for our time, and one that isn't easily answered. James talks about people being sick, and he seems to be prescribing a pathway to healing that is all but guaranteed. What are we to make of this? Is it simply a matter of asking the leaders of the church to anoint the sick person with oil (see James 5:14)?

James has no doubt that our prayers can be amazingly effective (see James 5:15–16). He boils it down to this equation:

- If a person who is righteous before God (the kind of person who has the vibrant faith we've been talking about through this book)

- prays earnestly and honestly to God,

- the prayer will be effective in that it will evoke God's response, drawing that person to Him, even if God gives an answer that is different than what the person is hoping for.

If your prayers seem weak and ineffectual, it may be due to a weak and ineffectual faith. A mature faith prays with the ultimate and underlying request that God's perfect will be done in your life, whether or not His will is aligned with your preferences. And you must always keep in mind that although God can heal both physically and spiritually, your spiritual health is His top priority.

So can sickness be caused by sin? Absolutely. Besides the sickness that arises from risky sinful behavior, there is the sickness that sometimes comes from disobedience (see 1 Corinthians 11:27–30). But because sin is not always the cause of sickness, we should be very careful about assigning blame for sickness of any kind. The disciples tried this once, and Jesus scolded them for it (see John 9:1–5). More than likely, you won't be able to identify the origin of the sickness and suffering you are going through, but that shouldn't stop you from realizing that God can use your affliction for His purposes (see 2 Corinthians 12:7–10).

That is why, for Christ's sake, I delight in weaknesses, in insults, in hardships, in persecutions, in difficulties. For when I am weak, then I am strong.

2 CORINTHIANS 12:10

- Instead of feeling bad that people of faith seem to be suffering more than others, feel bad for the suffering of people who have no faith.

- Christianity is the only religion that has an answer for sickness and suffering.

- Getting through your troubles begins with bringing God into them.

- Effective prayer begins with seeking God's answer, not yours.

- Knowing that God can use your affliction for His purposes is the first step toward healing.

The prayer of a righteous person is powerful and effective.

JAMES 5:16

FORTY-ONE

How to Pray with Power

We've been talking with a lot of people recently, from highly educated academics to run-of-the-mill people like the rest of us, doing our best to get a handle on the most effective way to navigate through these changing and challenging times. Since most of the people we talk with are Christians, it stands to reason that the advice revolves primarily around God and the Bible. We couldn't agree more. If God is real and the Bible is His Word, then those of us who claim to know and trust and follow Him need to track the playbook for life, especially when life gets tough.

But is it enough to believe that God exists and that the Bible is true? In a word, no. It's not enough. As we have been learning, faith alone in God alone is enough for starting a relationship with God, but it's not enough to navigate skillfully through life. You can't be passive. You have to take responsibility for your spiritual condition, drawing upon heavenly wisdom and doing those things God wants you to do: helping the disadvantaged, keeping your tongue under control, submitting yourself to God, and persevering through your sorrow and suffering. And most of all, you need to pray.

Prayer is the most underrated activity that any person of faith can be involved in. It's also the most powerful. Here are two reasons why:

- *Prayer brings you into God's presence.* Conversing with God takes you out of your humdrum world and connects you with the creator of the universe. And it happens immediately. You'll never be put on hold when you call on God through prayer. When you pray, you are immediately in God's presence.

Let us then approach God's throne of grace with confidence, so that we may receive mercy and find grace to help us in our time of need.
HEBREWS 4:16

- *Prayer changes your attitude and focus.* As we pray earnestly, we begin to align ourselves with God's plans rather than our own. We begin to let go of the death grip we have on our own desires, and we begin to subordinate what we want for what He wants. In our prayers, we make God the focal point of our life, so we change from being self-centered to being God-centered.

This is the confidence we have in approaching God: that if we ask anything according to his will, he hears us.

1 JOHN 5:14

So what should you pray for? John MacArthur teaches that prayer is drawn partly from the urgency of human needs and partly from the promises and challenges of God's Word. In other words, we need to present our needs to God. Of course, He knows what they are, but He wants to hear from us that we need His help. It's not necessary to plead, but simply to admit that God is the source of all we have and the answer to every problem. Prayer is acknowledging that God's sovereign rule over the universe He created includes even the small stuff in our own lives. There's nothing too big for God, but neither is anything too insignificant for Him.

Prayer is like a muscle. If it goes unused, it begins to atrophy. On the other hand, as you exercise your faith muscle and it grows stronger, the force of your prayers will grow stronger as well. History is filled with the stories of faithful people who prayed tirelessly for God to move in the lives of individuals, neighborhoods, nations, and the world. It's likely that such a person of prayer has petitioned God on your behalf, whether you know it or not.

If you desire to pray with that kind of power, you don't have to be a powerful person. You just have to be faithful to God and His Word. God desires to do mighty things in you, your neighborhood, your nation, and your world. But He needs you to pray! As the great prayer warrior E. M. Bounds has written: "Men and women are needed whose prayers will give to the world the utmost power of God; who will make His promises to blossom with rich and full results. God is waiting to hear us and challenges us to bring Him to do this thing by our praying."[2]

- Prayer can change a lot of things, but it is most likely to change you.

- You can pray for anything if you have a heart for God and believe that He will answer.

- Prayer is part of the process God uses to work in our lives.

- If you want to move a mountain with your prayers, focus on God, not the mountain.

- Prayer is simply talking with a personal God who loves you, knows you, and knows what's best for you.

My brothers and sisters, if one of you should wander from the truth and someone should bring that person back, remember this: Whoever turns a sinner from the error of their way will save them from death and cover over a multitude of sins.

JAMES 5:19–20

FORTY-TWO

BRING BACK A WANDERING SOUL

John Donne, the well-known seventeenth-century poet and pastor, was a deeply spiritual writer who spent a lot of time meditating on the idea of true faith—something we ourselves have been spending a lot of time thinking about in this book. In perhaps his most well-known poem—actually it's a meditation—Donne penned these immortal words: "No man is an island, entire of itself; every man is a piece of the continent, a part of the main. . . . Any man's death diminishes me, because I am involved in mankind, and therefore never send to know for whom the bell tolls; it tolls for thee."

There are no more appropriate words for this final chapter, except for the words of scripture itself, on this incredibly important idea: all of us who have been chosen by God to follow Him, and have responded with true belief, are part of one spiritual community.

When one of us, particularly someone we know, "wanders from the truth," it affects us all. We can never get by with saying, "Well, too bad about Jim. But better him than me." We have a responsibility before God to "bring that person back." If the wandering souls turn "from the error of their way," they will be saved from death.

This isn't a physical death as much as it is a spiritual death, but in either case it is a death that diminishes us all. And to be clear, we're not talking about someone who leaves your church to attend another, or even someone who has questions about God and his or her faith. We need to make lots of room for others to express their doubts, because we've all been there, and we may be there again.

No, this is something much more serious with far greater consequences. James is referring to people who have wandered from the *truth*. They have lost sight—sometimes through ignorance and at other times because of willful disobedience—and their lifestyle is seriously off kilter.

In these changing times, when many of us are facing new and ongoing pressures, we are tempted to forget about the "other guy" and stick to our own business. But God wants us demonstrate true faith and take responsibility for one another. This isn't about one person being morally superior to another (remember how much God detests pride), and it certainly isn't about one of us judging the other. This is about holding one another accountable to the truth.

James is reminding us that we are called to a higher standard of moral purity while maintaining a heart of forgiveness. When we live by this standard, we are God's true children, combining both faith and actions in a way that glorifies Him and encourages each other.

. . .FOR CHANGING TIMES

- Those who think they can live a life of faith alone eventually pay a price for their isolation.

- When we take responsibility for one another, we all benefit. When we don't, we all suffer.

- At the bottom of every mistake in behavior is a mistake in belief.

- We can't hold each other accountable unless we hold each other accountable to the truth.

NOTES

1. Sarah Pulliam Bailey, "Joni Eareckson Tada on Something Greater than Healing," *Christianity Today*, October 2010, http://www.christianitytoday.com/ct/2010/october/12.30.html.

2. E. M. Bounds, *Weapon of Prayer*. Quoted at http://www.goodreads.com/author/quotes/94390.E_M_Bounds.

ABOUT BRUCE AND STAN

Bruce Bickel is an attorney, but he hopes he doesn't stay that way. Bruce and his wife, Cheryl, live in the Seattle area.

Stan Jantz was involved in Christian retail for 25 years before venturing into marketing and publishing. Stan and his wife, Karin, live in Orange County, California.

Bruce and Stan have cowritten more than 50 books, including the international bestseller *God Is in the Small Stuff*. Their passion is to present truth in a correct, clear, and casual manner that encourages people to connect in a meaningful way with the living God.

Be sure to check out Bruce and Stan's website: www.Christianity101online.com.

Bruce and Stan are the cofounders of ConversantLife.com, a content and social media online experience designed to promote conversations about faith and culture. They encourage you to check out this site for stimulating blogs, videos, podcasts, and news.

If you have any questions or comments, you can connect with Bruce and Stan at info@Christianity101online.com.